The Quotable Feast

Bon Appetit!

Sarah E. Parvis

The Quotable Feast

Savory Sayings on Cooking, Eating, Drinking, and Entertaining

Sarah E. Parvis

A Stonesong Press Book

**Andrews McMeel
Publishing**

Kansas City

01 02 03 04 05 CTP 10 9 8 7 6 5 4 3 2 1

Library of Congress Cataloging-in-Publication Data
The quotable feast : savory sayings on cooking, eating, drinking, and entertaining / [compiled by] Sarah E. Parvis.
     p. cm.
   "A Stonesong Press book."
   ISBN 0-7407-1878-9
    1. Food—Quotations, maxims, etc. 2. Cookery—Quotations, maxims, etc. 3. Gastronomy—Quotations, maxims, etc. I. Parvis, Sarah E.

PN6084.F6 Q685 2001
641.3—dc21   2001022652

Book design by Lisa Martin
Illustrations by Susy Pilgrim Waters

For Jocelyn Ingham

Contents

Acknowledgments

My many thanks go to all the friends who have shared delicious meals with me and whose company has made the dining even better. To name a few: Cristina Capello, Ariane Barbanell, Ianthe Demos, David Solomon, Fritz Claudia, Peter Gudwin, Daniel Capuzzi, and Crystal Suggs. Thank you all for putting up with me as I agonized over finding the most appropriate description of an artichoke. I heartily thank those who shared with me their favorite words and thoughts about cooking, dining, and the pleasures of food, especially Pam Pezzoli and Mick Cribben. I am also grateful to Alison Fargis, Ellen Scordato, and Paul Fargis at the Stonesong Press and Jean Z. Lucas at Andrews McMeel Publishing.

And most of all, thank you to my family for your love and support.

Introduction

Everyone's ideas about culinary perfection grow and change as they wind through the years. At eight, perfection in the kitchen was undoubtedly hot dogs with macaroni and cheese, along with a healthy dose of ice cream or a Twix bar. In college, my own personal (and completely improvised) recipe for calzones was unparalleled in my mind, and the mere thought of the *panna cotta* I savored in Florence can make my taste buds dance the jig. There have been other standouts at different places and times: coffee and a buttery biscuit eaten outside in the summertime; the brie and roasted garlic appetizer at the Beech Tree Grill in Poughkeepsie, New York; a mushroom-smothered steak in Paris; a late-night bacon, egg, and cheese sandwich at a diner with friends; or mashed potatoes and gravy at the Thanksgiving table. From time to time, we try to put the joy of these meals into words. Just describing our cravings and memorable dishes can make our mouths water. I hope that the praise for eating, drinking, and dining in the following pages will do the same for you. There is no better way to stir the imagination and whet the appetite, so sit back, relax, and enjoy a quotable feast.

Kitchen
Inspiration

The Art of Cooking

"Poultry is for the cook what canvas is to the painter."
—*Anthelme Brillat-Savarin*

"My mother was a good recreational cook, but what she basically believed about cooking was that if you worked hard and prospered, someone else would do it for you."
—*Nora Ephron*

"We owe much to the fruitful meditation of our sages, but a sane view of life is, after all, elaborated mainly in the kitchen."
—*Joseph Conrad*

"Americans, more than any other culture on earth, are cookbook cooks; we learn to make our meals not from any oral tradition, but from a text. The just-wed cook brings to the new household no carefully copied collection of the family's cherished recipes, but a spanking new edition of *Fannie Farmer* or the *Joy of Cooking*."
—*John Thorne*

"Life is too short to stuff a mushroom."
—*Shirley Conran,* Superwoman, 1975

"The vision of milk and honey, it comes and goes.
But the odor of cooking goes on forever."
—*E. B. White,* One Man's Meat, 1944

"There is no technique, there is just the way to do it.
Now, are we going to measure or are we going to cook!"
—*Frances Mayes,* Under the Tuscan Sun, 1996

"Carve a ham as if you were shaving the face of a
friend."
—*Henri Charpentier*

"For me, the cooking life has been a long love affair,
with moments both sublime and ridiculous."
—*Anthony Bourdain,* Kitchen Confidential, 2000

"And now with some pleasure I find that it's seven; and
must cook dinner."
—*Virginia Woolf*

"A kitchen condenses the universe."
—*Betty Fussell,* My Kitchen Wars, *1999*

"It's a smell that arises from something as basic as wheat, as resourceful as the human hand and as powerful as fire."
—*Molly O'Neill, on the aroma of baking bread, in the* New York Times, *June 25, 1995*

"No artist can work simply for results; he must also *like* the work of getting them. . . . If a man has never been pleasantly surprised at the way the custard sets or flour thickens, there is not much hope of making a cook of him."
—*Robert Farrar Capon*

"Grilling, broiling, barbecuing—whatever you want to call it—is an art, not just a matter of building a pyre and throwing on a piece of meat as a sacrifice to the gods of the stomach."
—*James Beard,* Beard on Food, *1974*

On lobsters:

"Although these are delicious, getting them out of their shells involves giving them quite a brutal going-over. The way I look at it, they never did anything to me (although they are quite nasty-looking, and I do not like the way they stare at you from those fish tanks when you come into the restaurant—it is quite rude). On the other hand, if they serve you just the good parts already removed from the shell, that is quite a different matter, since the element of personal participation in the massacre is eliminated."

—*Miss Piggy, in* Miss Piggy's Guide to Life
(as Told to Henry Beard), *1981*

"The dangerous person in the kitchen is the one who goes rigidly by weights, measurements, thermometers, and scales."

—*X. Marcel Boulestin*

"The discovery of a new dish does more for the happiness of mankind than the discovery of a star."

—*Anthelme Brillat-Savarin,* Physiologie du Goût, *1825*

"Governing a great nation is like cooking a small dish—too much handling will spoil it."

—*Lao-tzu*

"Grilling is like sunbathing. Everyone knows it is bad for you but no one ever stops doing it."

—*Laurie Colwin,* Home Cooking, *1988*

"Poultry is like meat, except when you cook it rare. Then it's like bird-flavored Jell-O."

—*P. J. O'Rourke*

"To cookery, we owe well-ordered States
Assembling man in dear society
. . . The art of cookery drew us gently forth
From that ferocious life when, void of faith,
The Anthropophagian ate his brother."

—*Hesiod*

"Let onions lurk within the bowl
And, scarce-suspected, animate the whole."

—*Sydney Smith, "Recipe for Salad," in Lady S. Holland's*
A Memoir of the Reverend Sydney Smith, *1855*

"Prepared and fast foods have given us the time and freedom to see cooking as an art form, a form of creative expression."

—*Jeff Smith,* The Frugal Gourmet Keeps the Feast, *1995*

On the best way to thaw a frozen turkey:
"Blow in his ear."

—*Johnny Carson*

"What I love about cooking is that after a hard day, there is something comforting about the fact that if you melt butter and add flour and then hot stock, *it will get thick!* It's a sure thing! It's a sure thing in a world where nothing is sure; it has a mathematical certainty in a world where those of us who long for some kind of certainty are forced to settle for crossword puzzles."

—*Nora Ephron*

"Cooking is a great form of stress relief."

—*Queen Latifah*

"When *I'm* a Duchess . . . I won't have any pepper in my kitchen *at all*. Soup does very well without—Maybe it's always pepper that makes people hot-tempered . . . and vinegar that makes them sour—and chamomile that makes them bitter—and—and barley-sugar and such that make children sweet-tempered. I only wish people knew *that*: then they wouldn't be so stingy about it."

—*Lewis Carroll*, Alice's Adventures in Wonderland, *1865*

"My wife does wonderful things with leftovers—she throws them out."

—*Herb Shriner*, Reader's Digest, *1956*

"It's you and your barbeque against all of the other barbeques. Do you want the other barbeques in the neighborhood to kick sand on yours? It's a team effort. Do your part."

—*Jody Maroni, in Brigit Binn's*
Jody Maroni's Sausage Kingdom Cookbook, *1997*

"Cooking is a serious matter, but it should also be fun."

—*Maria Floris*

"Food that's beautiful to look at seems to taste better than food that isn't."

—*Emeril Lagasse,* Emeril's New
New Orleans Cooking, *1993*

"What better way to celebrate a new millennium, a new century, and a new year than to revisit historic barbecuing and grilling in its modern forms?"

—*George Foreman,* George Foreman's Big Book
of Grilling, Barbecue, and Rotisserie, *2000*

"I cooked once in 1978 and decided it was a bad idea."

—*M. G. Lord*

"I prefer my oysters fried; that way I know my oysters died."

—*Roy Blount Jr.*

"By November I had convinced myself that I had better things to do than read *Moby-Dick* and learn about the Continental Congress. Cook, for instance."

—*Ruth Reichl,* Tender at the Bone, *1998*

"There is in every cook's opinion
No savoury dish without an onion:
But lest your kissing should be spoiled
The onion must be thoroughly boiled."

—Jonathan Swift

"There is no such thing as a little garlic."
—*Arthur Baer*

"I don't even butter my bread. I consider that cooking."
—*Katherine Cebrian*

"When men reach their sixties and retire, they go to pieces. Women go right on cooking."
—*Gail Sheehy*

"Nouvelle cuisine, roughly translated, means 'I can't believe I spent ninety-six dollars and I'm still hungry!'"
—*Mike Kalina*

"Fondue is out of style. It's like the leisure suit of the food world."
—*Juli Hess*

"I don't know much about the details of cooking— I mean, what's a 'twist' of lemon?"
—*Kool Moe Dee*

"Everyone has the talent to some degree: even making a peanut butter and jelly sandwich, you know whether it tastes better to you with raspberry jam or grape jelly; on chewy pumpernickel or white toast."

—*Anna Shapiro,* A Feast of Words, *1996*

"God sends meat, and the devil sends cooks."

—*John Taylor*

"Kissing don't last; cookery do!"

—*George Meredith*

"One can become a cook, but one is born a roaster of meat."

—*Anthelme Brillat-Savarin,*
Physiologie de Goût, *1825*

On his wife's cooking:
"How could toast have bones?"

—*Rodney Dangerfield*

"Cooking is like making music. The same way that you put a snare with this hi-hat and that foot, and you put this voice on top of this one, and combine them and the blend has a certain feel that's hard to describe. Cooking is the same thing. You might take salt, pepper, oil, potatoes, and onions. These different things together make a different taste."

—*Doug E. Fresh*

"The pot is less an implement of the home kitchen than its emblem—at least, of that room as it once was, dark and smoky, its walls coated with grease, and permeated with the smell of food. Because of this, the pot takes on an amorphous shape in our imagination, which is why it lends itself so easily to such compounds as *teapot* or *beanpot* or *potherb* or *potholder*. Or, for that matter, *crackpot, fusspot,* and *stinkpot*."

—*John Thorne,* Pot on the Fire, 2000

"I feel a recipe is only a theme, which an intelligent cook can play each time with a variation."

—*Madame Benoit*

"When compelled to cook, I produce a meal that would make a sword swallower gag."

—*Russell Baker*

"No mean woman can cook well, for it called for a light head, a generous spirit, and a large heart."

—*Paul Gauguin*

"We're not building a rocket ship here, we're cooking— plain and simple."

—*Emeril Lagasse,* Emeril's TV Dinners, *1998*

"As all cooks know, ingredients of the moment are the best guides."

—*Frances Mayes,* Under the Tuscan Sun, *1996*

"An idealist is one who, on noticing that a rose smells better than a cabbage, concludes that it will also make a better soup."

—*H. L. Mencken*

"I can't cook. I use a smoke alarm as a timer."
—*Carol Siskind*

"To make the best of all possible chilis can become
an obsession."
—*George Lang*, Nobody Knows
the Truffles I've Seen, 1998

On nouvelle cuisine:
"It's toy food. Feed it to toy people."
—*Jeff Smith*

"Line cooking done well is a beautiful thing to watch.
It's a high-speed collaboration resembling, at its best,
ballet or modern dance."
—*Anthony Bourdain*, Kitchen Confidential, 2000

"When I'm old and gray, I want to have a house by the
sea. And paint. With a lot of wonderful chums, good
music and booze around. And a damn good kitchen to
cook in."
—*Ava Gardner*

"Real-man cooking leads to discoveries like my nutritional bombshells. Cooking by recipes doesn't. Who would guess that a peanut-butter-and-bacon sandwich is so good it will bring tears to your eyes? It does. Add lettuce, and you have a complete meal, with every known daily nutrient needed by the average 200-pound man."

—*Roger Welsch,* Diggin' In and Piggin' Out, *1997*

"Cooking drunk was as dangerous as driving."

—*Ruth Reichl,* Tender at the Bone, *1998*

"When microwave ovens didn't exist . . . did people sit around . . . saying, 'Heat is so boring. I wish we could bombard a potato with mutant intergalactic energy?'"

—*Colin McEnroe*

"We may live without friends; we may live without books; but civilized man cannot live without cooks."

—*Edward Bulwer-Lytton*

"I idolized my mother. I didn't realize she was a lousy cook until I went into the army."

—*Jackie Gayle*

"Once I've made something, I don't feel like eating it. The fun is in making it."

—*Heavy D*

"Men cook more, and we all know why. It is the only interesting household task."

—*Nora Ephron*

"Men do not have to cook their food; they do so for symbolic reasons to show they are men and not beasts."

—*Edmund Leach*

"Do not make a stingy sandwich
Pile the cold-cuts high
Customers should see the salami
Coming through the rye."

—*Allan Sherman*

"Nobody can cook as well as mother."

—*Maria Floris*

"According to the Spanish proverb, four persons are wanted to make a good salad: a spendthrift for oil, a miser for vinegar, a counselor for salt, and a madman to stir it all up."

—*Abraham Hayward*

"I no longer prepare food or drink with more than one ingredient."

—*Cyra McFadden*

On nouvelle cuisine:
"It's so beautifully arranged, you know someone's fingers have been all over it."

—*Julia Child, in the*
San Francisco Chronicle, *1982*

"I refuse to believe that trading recipes is silly. Tuna-fish casserole is at least as real as corporate stock."

—*Barbara Grizzuti Harrison*

"Every girl should know how to make gefilte fish."
—*Ruth Reichl,* Tender at the Bone, *1998*

"About all I can make is a bag of chips open."
—*Grandmaster Flash*

"When social revolutions hustled women out of the kitchen and into the boardroom, I seemed to be caught *in flagrante* with a potholder in my hand."
—*Betty Fussell,* My Kitchen Wars, *1999*

Never Trust a Skinny Cook

OURSINS

gâteaux

GÂTEAUX

Lavande

citron

pain

Chefs Great and Small

"Where you find in the kitchen a light cleaver, a heavy knife with a straight, sharp edge, and a spacious mincing board of hard wood, you may be certain that you are in the home of a chef."

—*Angelo Pellegrini,* The Unprejudiced Palate, 1948

"Noncooks think it's silly to invest two hours' work in two minutes' enjoyment; but if cooking is evanescent, well, so is ballet."

—*Julia Child*

"'Tis an ill cook that cannot lick his own fingers."

—*William Shakespeare,* Romeo and Juliet, 1594

"Cookery has become an art, a noble science; cooks are gentlemen."

—*Robert Burton,* The Anatomy of Melancholy, 1621

"I like a cook who smiles out loud when he tastes his own work. Let God worry about your modesty; I want to see your enthusiasm."

—*Robert Farrar Capon*

"Some people's food always tastes better than others, even if they are cooking the same dish at the same dinner. Now I will tell you why—because one person has more life in them—more fire, more vitality, more guts—than others. A person without these things can never make food taste right, no matter what materials you give them, it is no use."

—*Rosa Lewis*

"If you subtract Elizabeth David from the scene . . . you have just foothills, there is no mountain."

—*Alan Davidson, on England's premier chef, in the* International Herald Tribune, *June 1, 1992*

"The true cook is the perfect blend, the only perfect blend, of an artist and philosopher. He knows his worth: he holds in his palm the happiness of mankind, the welfare of generations yet unborn."

—*Norman Douglas*

"I developed the asbestos skin of a cook, stirring the pans with my fingers if there were no handy spoons and occasionally forgetting a potholder before reaching into the oven. I learned to ignore minor burns. And to improvise: my mother's kitchen was ill-equipped, so I used a wine bottle for a rolling pin and beat egg whites with a forty-year-old eggbeater."

—*Ruth Reichl,* Tender at the Bone, *1998*

"Our lives are not in the lap of the gods, but in the lap of our cooks."

—*Lin Yutang,* The Importance of Living, *1937*

"After eating, an *epicure* gives a thin smile of satisfaction; a *gastronome,* burping into his napkin, praises the food in a magazine; a *gourmet,* repressing his burp, criticizes the food in the same magazine; a *gourmand* belches happily and tells everybody where he ate; a *glutton* embraces the white porcelain altar, or more plainly, he barfs."

—*William Safire*

On eating his first oyster:
"I'd learned something. Viscerally, instinctively, spiritually—even in some small precursive way, sexually—and there was no turning back. The genie was out of the bottle. My life as a cook, and as a chef, had begun.

"Food had power.

"It could inspire, astonish, shock, excite, delight and impress. It had the power to please me . . . and others. This was valuable information."

—*Anthony Bourdain,* Kitchen Confidential, *2000*

"'My instructions are in my fingers. I know what secret ingredients to put in just by using my nose!' And she was slicing with such ferocity, seemingly inattentive to her sharp cleaver, that I was afraid her fingertips would become one of the ingredients of the red-cooked eggplant and shredded pork dish."

—*Amy Tan,* The Joy Luck Club, *1989*

"A gourmet who thinks of calories is like a tart who looks at her watch."

—*James Beard*

"Any cook should be able to run the country."
—*Vladimir I. Lenin, as quoted in Alexander Solzhenitsyn's* The First Circle, *1968*

"What did one do with fenugreek? I didn't know, nor did anyone else, but we all had a bottle of it, we apprentice gourmets, in our spice racks."
—*Mary Cantwell,* Manhattan, When I Was Young, *1995*

"Maybe we should put the chefs of the world in charge of the wars!

"I can see it now. The battle is about to take place in a great banquet hall. There is an enormous cooking center in the middle of the hall, bleachers filled with spectators seated all around.

"The battle begins: 'I'll see your sauce and raise you an artichoke!'"
—*Jeff Smith,* The Frugal Gourmet Keeps the Feast, *1995*

"A good cook is like a sorceress who dispenses happiness."
—*Elsa Schiaparelli*

"Speaking for myself, I can definitely throw it down in the kitchen and I'm no chef!"

—*Queen Latifah*

"There is a great difference in my mind between innocence in this gourmand interpretation, and ignorance. The one presupposes the other, and yet a truly innocent cook or host is never guilty of the great sin of pretension, while many an ignorant one errs hideously in this direction."

— *M. F. K. Fisher, "I Is for Innocence,"*
An Alphabet for Gourmets, *1949*

"I want to tell you about the dark recesses of the restaurant underbelly—a subculture whose centuries-old militaristic hierarchy and ethos of 'rum, buggery and the lash' make for a mix of unwavering order and nerve-shattering chaos—because I find it all quite comfortable, like a nice warm bath."

—*Anthony Bourdain,* Kitchen Confidential, *2000*

"Go into the kitchen to shake the chef's hand. If he is thin, have second thoughts about eating there; if he is thin and sad, flee."

—Fernand Point, in the NEW YORK TIMES, July 10, 1986

"There has always been a food processor in the kitchen, but once upon a time she was usually called the missus, or Mom."

—*Sue Berkman*

"Once I grew a mustache in an attempt to look like a cook."

—*George Lang,* Nobody Knows the Truffles I've Seen, *1998*

"A gourmet is just a glutton with brains."

—*Philip W. Haberman Jr., "How to Be a Calorie Chiseler,"* Vogue, *January 15, 1961*

"A man who loves good food has a way of making it gravitate toward his kitchen."

—*Angelo Pellegrini,* The Unprejudiced Palate, *1948*

"A good cook is a certain slow poisoner, if you are not temperate."

—*Voltaire, "Poisonings,"* Philosophical Dictionary, *1764*

"Woe to the cook whose sauce has no sting."

—*Chaucer*

"It is the sauce that distinguishes a good chef. The *saucier* is a soloist in the orchestra of a great kitchen."

—*Fernand Point*

"A master cook! why he's the man of men,
For a professor; he designs, he draws,
He paints, he carves, he builds, he fortifies,
Makes citadels of curious fowl and fish.
Some he dry-ditches, some moats round with broths,
Mounts marrow-bones, cuts fifty angled custards,
Rears bulwark pies; and for his outer works,
He raiseth ramparts of immortal crust,
And teacheth all the tactics at one dinner—
What ranks, what files to put his dishes in,
The whole art military!"

—*Ben Johnson*

"My feet have felt the toil of years on hard kitchen floors, and when one meets another cook one exchanges more foot balm panaceas than recipes."

—*Clarissa Dickson Wright,* Food, *1999*

"A good cook is the peculiar gift of the gods. He must be a perfect creature from the brain to the palate, from the palate to the finger's end."

—*Walter Savage Landor, "Anacreon and Polycrates,"*
Imaginary Conversations, 1828

"Bad cooks—and the utter lack of reason in the kitchen—have delayed human development longest and impaired it most."

—*Friedrich Nietzsche,* Beyond Good and Evil, 1886

"It is true that taste for unfamiliar food and drink can be cultivated, as it is true that matters of taste cannot be settled by argument. Here, too, it is possible to exaggerate and to be duped by gastronomic nincompoops who write of gourmets with a sense of taste so refined that they can tell whether a fish was caught under or between the bridges, and distinguish by its superior flavor the thigh on which the partridge leans while asleep."

—*Angelo Pellegrini,* The Unprejudiced Palate, 1948

The Soul of Cooking

Essential Ingredients

"Beef is the soul of cooking."

—*Marie Antoine Carême*

"Herbs and spices are the soul of your kitchen . . ."
—*Isabel Allende,* Aphrodite: A Memoir of the Senses, *1998*

"Bread is like dresses, hats and shoes—in other words, essential!"

—*Emily Post*

"A cheese may disappoint. It may be dull, it may be naive, it may be oversophisticated. Yet it remains cheese, milk's leap toward immortality."
—*Clifton Fadiman,* Any Number Can Play, *1957*

"Potatoes are to food what sensible shoes are to fashion."

—*Linda Wells*

"A kitchen without a lemon is like a song without a tune."
—*David Wheeler, "A Cultivated Table,"*
Country Life, *January 19, 1995*

"Pray for peace and grace and spiritual food,
For wisdom and guidance, for all these are good,
But don't forget the potatoes."

—*John Tyler Pettee*

"Bread is the king of the table, and all else is merely the court that surrounds the king. The countries are the soup, the meat, the vegetables, the salad . . . but bread is king."

—*Louis Bromfield*

"Cheese is probably the friendliest of foods. It endears itself to everything and never tires of showing off to great advantage. Any liquor or, I may say, any potable or any edible loves to be seen in the company of cheese. Naturally, some nationalities choose one type of companion and some another, but you very seldom find clashes of temperament in passing."

—*James Beard*

On garlic:
"My final, considered judgment is that the hardy bulb
blesses and ennobles everything it touches—with the
possible exception of ice cream and pie."
—*Angelo Pellegrini,* The Unprejudiced Palate, *1948*

"Salt is the policeman of taste: it keeps the various
flavors of a dish in order, and restrains the stronger
from tyrannizing over the weaker."
—*Malcolm de Chazal*

"Mutton is the meat I love.
On the dresser see it lie;
Oh, the charming white and red;
Finer meat ne'er met the eye."
—*Jonathan Swift*

"Talk of joy: there may be things better than beef stew
and baked potatoes and home-made bread—there
may be."
—*David Grayson,* Adventures in Contentment, *1907*

"Blues is to jazz what yeast is to bread—without it, it's flat."

—*Carmen McRae*

"What I say is, if a man really likes potatoes, he must be a pretty decent sort of fellow."

—*A. A. Milne*

"Everything you see I owe to spaghetti."

—*Sophia Loren*

"We lived very simply—but with all the essentials of life well understood and provided for—hot baths, cold champagne, new peas and old brandy."

—*Winston S. Churchill, in* The Last Lion, *by William Manchester, 1983*

"Chicken salad has a certain glamour about it. Like the little black dress, it is chic and adaptable anywhere."

—*Laurie Colwin,* Home Cooking, *1988*

"If I had to say what one ingredient
I must have in the kitchen, it would
be the lemon because the flavor, both
assertive and enhancing, is like liquid
sunshine going into food."

—Frances Mayes, BELLA TUSCANY, 1999

"Everyone's got an opinion when it comes to how to cook 'perfect' corn on the cob, but the truth is that the corn itself is the most important factor rather than the cooking method and timing. The fresher the corn, the better it will be."

—*John Hadamuscin,* John Hadamuscin's Down Home, *1993*

"Of all smells, bread; of all tastes, salt."

—*George Herbert*

"The true essentials of a feast are only food and feed."

—*Oliver Wendell Holmes*

"All the ingenious men, and all the scientific men, and all the imaginative men in the world could never invent, if all their wits were boiled into one, anything so curious and so ridiculous as the lobster."

—*Charles Kingsley*

"A man who is stingy with saffron is capable of seducing his own grandmother."

—*Norman Douglas*

"The strands of spaghetti were vital, almost alive in my mouth, and the olive oil was singing with flavor. It was hard to imagine that four simple ingredients [pasta, garlic, cheese, and olive oil] could marry so perfectly."

—*Ruth Reichl,* Tender at the Bone, *1998*

"Bread was not only a staple, but was also almost sacred in our home, almost godlike . . ."

—*George Lang,* Nobody Knows the Truffles I've Seen, *1998*

"As for butter versus margarine, I trust cows more than chemists."

—*Joan Dye Gussow*

"A kiss without a mustache, they said then, is like an egg without salt; I will add to it: and it is like Good without Evil."

—*Jean-Paul Sartre*

"Pepper is small in quantity and great in virtue."

—*Plato*

"No cook should ever be without garlic, parsley, onion, and celery. I have listed them in the order of absolute necessity."

—*Angelo Pellegrini,* The Unprejudiced Palate, *1948*

"Unbuttered toast is a substance half complete, and to be forced to eat it in that state is necessarily to feel deprived."

—*John Thorne,* Pot on the Fire, *2000*

"If toast always lands butter side down and cats always land on their feet, what happens if you strap toast on the back of a cat and drop it?"

—*Steven Wright*

"The forms of government fall when it comes up to the question of bread—bread for the family, something to eat. Bread to a man with a hungry family comes first—before his union, before his citizenship, before his church affiliation. Bread!"

—*John L. Lewis*

"Salt is white and pure,—there is something holy in salt."

—Nathaniel Hawthorne, Passages from the American Notebooks, *1868*

"A bowl of soup, some rye bread, some OJ and boom! Your body loves you! If you really want it to love you, eat this with water. If you really really want it to love you, go for a walk afterwards."

—KRS-One

"There are four unbroken rules when it comes to Thanksgiving: there must be turkey and dressing, cranberries, mashed potatoes, and pumpkin pie."

—John Hadamuscin, John Hadamuscin's Down Home, *1993*

"There is nothing like soup. It is by nature eccentric: no two are ever alike, unless of course you get your soup in a can."

—Laurie Colwin, Home Cooking, *1988*

"If ever I had to practice cannibalism, I might manage
if there were enough tarragon around."

—*James Beard, in the* New York Times,
January 24, 1985

"Parsley—the jewel of herbs, both in the pot and on
the plate."

—*Albert Stockli*

Unappeasable Hunger

The Power of Appetite

"For nothing keeps a poet
in his high singing mood
like unappeasable hunger
for unattainable food."

—*Joyce Kilmer*

"L'appétit vient en mangeant." (The appetite grows by
eating.)

—*François Rabelais,* Gargantua and Pantagruel, *1532*

"If thou rise with an Appetite, thou art sure never to sit
down without one."

—*William Penn*

"He who wants to eat cannot sleep."

—*Anthelme Brillat-Savarin*

"He who is a slave to the belly seldom worships God."

—*Saadī*

"The way one thinks on a diet is the way people in famine think about food—obsessively, with great care—but turned upside down."
—*Sallie Tisdale,* The Best Thing I Ever Tasted, *2000*

"When things get particularly trying or my schedule is hectic (which is always!), I would eat to soothe my frazzled soul, but seldom to satisfy my hunger."
—*Sarah Ferguson, Duchess of York,*
Dining with the Duchess, *1998*

"Appetite, an universal wolf."
—*William Shakespeare,* Troilus and Cressida, *1603*

"There is no such things as bad bread when you have a good appetite."
—*Gabriel García Márquez*

"He who eats for two must work for three."
—*Kurdish proverb*

"Just as every king, prophet, warrior, and saint has a mother, so every Napoleon, every Einstein, every Jesus has to eat."

—*Betty Fussell,* My Kitchen Wars, *1999*

"The belly is the reason why man does not mistake himself for a God."

—*Friedrich Nietzsche*

"and i taste in my natural appetite
the bond of live things everywhere."

—*Lucille Clifton, from "Cutting Greens"*

"Undoubtedly, the desire for food has been, and still is, one of the main causes of great political events."

—*Bertrand Russell*

"You'll be hungry again in an hour."

—*Message in a fortune cookie opened by Ziggy
in the cartoon "Ziggy," created by Tom Wilson*

"The poor seek food, the rich seek an appetite."

—*Hindu proverb*

"No amount of political freedom will satisfy the hungry masses."

—*Vladimir I. Lenin*

"Hungry men have no respect for law, authority, or human life."

—*Marcus Garvey*

"The best sauce in the world is hunger."

—*Miguel de Cervantes*

"In the Lord's Prayer, the first petition is for daily bread. No one can worship God or love his neighbor on an empty stomach."

—*Woodrow Wilson*

"Honest bread is very well—it's the butter that makes the temptation."

—*Douglas Jerrold*

"To a man with an empty stomach,
food is God."

—Mahatma Gandhi

"You first parents of the human race . . . who ruined yourself for an apple, what might you not have done for a truffled turkey?"

—*Anthelme Brillat-Savarin*

"The glutton digs his grave with his teeth."

—*English proverb*

"It is a hard matter, my fellow citizens, to argue with the belly, since it has no ears."

—*Plutarch*

"Now good digestion wait on appetite,
And health on both!"

—*William Shakespeare,* Macbeth, 1606

"In general, mankind, since the improvement of cookery, eats twice as much as nature requires."

—*Benjamin Franklin*

"We didn't starve, but we didn't eat chicken unless we were sick, or the chicken was."

—*Bernard Malamud*

"Hunger can explain many acts. It can be said that all vile acts are done to satisfy hunger."

—*Maxim Gorky*

"Hunger, like lust in action, is savage, extreme, rude, cruel."

—*Betty Fussell,* My Kitchen Wars, 1999

"When we lose, I eat. When we win, I eat. I also eat when it's rained out."

—*Tommy Lasorda*

"We have created amazing institutions and systems to satisfy our endlessly inventive hunger, but we are insatiable; we can't be filled, can't be done. This is the danger, the gift, one of the secrets of food."

—*Sallie Tisdale,* The Best Thing I Ever Tasted, 2000

"The great companies did not know that the line between hunger and anger is a thin line."

—*John Steinbeck*

"I eat merely to put food out of my mind."

—*N. F. Simpson,* The Hole, *1964*

"I am not a glutton—I am an explorer of food."

—*Erma Bombeck*

"What drives you to decide to make dolmades, a dish that requires hours and disappears in minutes? Like the power of a curse lifted—anyone who has ever tasted it is subject to an occasional greed and hunger that nothing else can satisfy. . . . Each one swallowed creates the need for another, an anxiety that there will not be enough. Since hours have been spent by not one cook but many, there is nothing to stop you from eating until you feel your stomach might burst."

—*Catherine Temma Davidson,* The Priest Fainted, *1998*

"My doctor told me to stop having intimate dinners for four. Unless there are three other people."

—*Orson Welles*

"'Tis not the meat, but 'tis the appetite makes eating a delight."

—*Sir John Suckling*

"Life itself is the proper binge."

—*Julia Child*

"Epicurean cooks
Sharpen with cloyless sauce his appetite."
—*William Shakespeare,* Antony and Cleopatra, 1607

"Love and business and family and religion and art and patriotism are nothing but shadows of words when a man's starving."

—*O. Henry*

"Appetite is the best sauce."

— Lady Bird Johnson,
A WHITE HOUSE DIARY, 1970

Warm Cookies and Cold Milk

The Solace of Food

"Warm cookies and cold milk are good for you."
—*Robert Fulghum*

"Food is our common ground, a universal experience."
—*James Beard,* Beard on Food, *1974*

"Next to jazz music, there is nothing that lifts the spirits and strengthens the soul more then a good bowl of chili."
—*Harry James*

"Tapioca is the teddy-bear of desserts, an edible security blanket."
—*Jane and Michael Stern,* Square Meals, *1984*

"Next to getting warm and keeping warm, dinner and supper were the most interesting things we had to think about. Our lives centered around warmth and food and the return of the men at nightfall."
—*Willa Cather*

"Toast was a big item in my mother's culinary pharma-
copeia. At first it was served plain and dry, but that was
soon followed by crisp, sweet cinnamon toast, then
baby-bland toast that tasted soothingly of fresh air.
Thick slices of French toast, crisp and golden outside
but moist and eggy within, would probably come next,
always topped with a melting knob of sweet butter and
a dusting of confectioner's sugar. I knew I was close to
recovery when I got the toast I liked best—almost-
burned rye bread toast covered with salt butter."

—*Mimi Sheraton*

"Chili's a lot like sex: When it's good it's great, and even
when it's bad, it's not so bad."

—*Bill Boldenweck, in* American Way, *June 1982*

"The smell of good bread baking, like the sound of
lightly flowing water, is indescribable in its evocation
of innocence and delight."

—*M. F. K. Fisher*

"There is nothing to which men, while they have food and drink, cannot reconcile themselves."

—*George Santayana,* Interpretations of
Poetry and Religion, *1900*

"Cake and pie and bread are dreamcatchers for me. German chocolate and Lady Baltimore are black-market drugs so rich with inaccurate sensations of maternal comfort and infantile security they take my breath away."

—*Sallie Tisdale,* The Best Thing I Ever Tasted, *2000*

"What is patriotism but the love of good things we ate in our childhood."

—*Lin Yutang*

"Seeing is deceiving. It's eating that's believing."

—*James Thurber,* Further Fables for Our Time, *1956*

"Do you have a kinder, more adaptable friend in the food world than soup?"

—*Miss Manners (Judith Martin)*

"A great step toward independence is a good-humoured stomach."

—*Seneca*

"All's well that ends with a good meal."

—*Arnold Lobel*

"O poor immortal comforts: fish, some bread and wine."

—*Nikos Kazantzakis*

"Before I was born my mother was in great agony of spirit and in a tragic situation. She could take no food except iced oysters and champagne. If people ask me when I began to dance, I reply, 'In my mother's womb, probably as a result of the oysters and champagne—the food of Aphrodite.'"

—*Isadora Duncan*

"I truly believe that juices have contributed more than anything else to my good health and optimistic outlook."

—*Jay Kordich,* The Juiceman's Power of Juicing, *1992*

"The secret of staying young is to live honestly, eat slowly, and lie about your age."

—Lucille Ball

"There is nothing better on a cold wintry day than a properly made pot pie."

—*Craig Claiborne*

"It may not be a dish for every occasion, but when it comes to those American foods that somehow always evoke casual warmth, wholesome relaxation, and good-will, a toothsome hash served with green salad, fresh bread, and a premium beer is still pretty hard to beat."

—*James Villas*

"Sir, respect your dinner: idolize it, enjoy it properly. You will be many hours in the week, many weeks in the year, and many years in your life happier if you do."

—*William M. Thackeray*

"Let food be your medicine and medicine be your food."

—*Hippocrates*

"A man may be a pessimistic determinist before lunch and an optimistic believer in the will's freedom after it."

—*Aldous Huxley, "Pascal," Do What You Will, 1929*

"The first thing I remember liking that liked me back was food."

—*Valerie Harper, on the 1970s TV show* Rhoda

"The hearty, discriminating eater is seldom a sour puss."

—*Angelo Pellegrini,* The Unprejudiced Palate, *1948*

"A man hath no better thing under the sun, than to eat, and to drink, and to be merry."

—*Ecclesiastes 8:15*

"Nowadays, food is not the enemy. I am not fearful of every forkful. Rather, I now use food as a way to control my life."

—*Sarah Ferguson, Duchess of York,*
Dining with the Duchess, *1998*

"A good meal makes a man feel more charitable toward the whole world than any sermon."

—*Arthur Pendenys*

"All happiness depends on a leisurely breakfast."

—*John Gunther,* Newsweek, *April 14, 1958*

"I believe I once considerably scandalized her by declaring that clear soup was a more important factor in life than a clear conscience."
—*Saki, "The Blind Spot," in* Beasts and Super Beasts, *1914*

"When a man's stomach is full it makes no difference whether he is rich or poor."
—*Euripides,* Electra, *413 B.C.*

"I live on good soup, not on fine words."
—*Molière*

"Unknowingly I had started sorting people by their tastes. Like a hearing child born of deaf parents, I was shaped by my mother's handicap, discovering that food could be a way of making sense of the world."
—*Ruth Reichl,* Tender at the Bone, *1998*

"He who distinguishes the true savor of food can never be a glutton; he who does not cannot be otherwise."
—*Henry David Thoreau*

"It is not really an exaggeration to say that peace and happiness begin, geographically, where garlic is used in cooking."

—*X. Marcel Boulestin*

"In the morning she was there as well, feeding me rice porridge flavored with chicken broth. She was feeding me this because I had the chicken pox and one chicken knew how to fight another."

—*Amy Tan,* The Joy Luck Club, *1989*

"He that eateth well, drinketh well; he that drinketh well, sleepeth well; he that sleepeth well, sinneth not; he that sinneth not goeth straight through Purgatory to Paradise."

—*William Lithgow,* The Rare Adventures and
Painefull Peregrinations, *1614*

"An army marches on its stomach."

—*Napoleon Bonaparte*

"Soups can cure any illness, whether physical or mental."
—*Laura Esquivel,* Like Water for Chocolate, *1989*

"Principles have no real force except when one is well fed."
—*Mark Twain*

"Serenely full, the epicure would say,
Fate cannot harm me, I have dined today."
—*Sydney Smith, in Lady S. Holland's*
A Memoir of the Reverend Sydney Smith, *1855*

Southern Biscuits
and Cajun Spices

Hot
Sauce

Ethnic Traditions
and Regional Delicacies

"The Mason-Dixon line is the dividing line between cold bread and hot biscuits."

—*Bob Taylor*

"Somewhere lives a bad Cajun cook, just as somewhere must live one last ivory-billed woodpecker. For me, I don't expect ever to encounter either one."

—*William Least Heat Moon,* Blue Highways, *1982*

"Tomatoes and oregano make it Italian; wine and tarragon make it French. Sour cream makes it Russian; lemon and cinnamon make it Greek. Soy sauce makes it Chinese; garlic makes it good."

—*Alice May Brock*

"I'm in favor of liberalizing immigration because of the effect it would have on restaurants. I'd let just about everybody in except the English."

—*Calvin Trillin*

"Grits is the first truly American food."

—*Turner Catledge*

"Eating in Germany is easy, because there is basically only one kind of food, called the 'wurst.'"

—*Dave Barry,* Dave Barry's Only Travel
Guide You'll Ever Need, *1991*

"The Chanukah buckwheat cake or *latke* is much thicker and smaller [than the pancake served in American restaurants] and does not deserve its name unless, when served, it is fairly dripping with fat. It would be futile to attempt a description of it here, for the glories of a successful Chanukah *latke* defy the resources of the richest of Gentile languages."

—*Abraham Cahan,* Grandma Never Lived in America, *1985*

"In Bordeaux, as in the rest of France, the marriage of food and wine is celebrating hundreds of years of happiness."

—*Florence Fabricant*

"How can you govern a country that has 246 varieties of cheese?"

—*Charles de Gaulle*

"As a Southerner, to me 'deep fried' is an enchanting phrase. We never met an artichoke, when I was growing up, except marinated in a jar."

—*Frances Mayes,* Bella Tuscany, *1999*

"I don't know whether or not Wisconsin has a cheese-tasting festival, but I who am a lover of cheese believe that it should. Cheese was everywhere, cheese centers, cheese cooperatives, cheese stores and stands, perhaps even cheese ice cream. I can believe anything since I saw a score of signs advertising Swiss Cheese Candy. Now I can't persuade anyone that it exists, that I did not make it up."

—*John Steinbeck,* Travels with Charley: In Search of America, *1962*

"Boiled cabbage à l'Anglaise is something compared with which steamed coarse newsprint bought from bankrupt Finnish salvage dealers and heated over smoky oil stoves is an exquisite delicacy."

—*"Cassandra" (William Connor)*

"The human body, when it freezes in eternal silence, is said to be worth about ninety-eight cents. The body of an ordinary south European, if we could devise the means for extracting the garlic from it, would be worth a bushel of gold."

—*Angelo Pellegrini,* The Unprejudiced Palate, *1948*

"Public and private food in America has become eatable, here and there extremely good. Only the fried potatoes go on unchanged, as deadly as before."

—*Luigi Barzini,* O America, *1977*

"France has found a unique way of controlling its unwanted critter population. They have done this by giving unwanted animals like snails, pigeons, and frogs fancy names, thus transforming common backyard pests into expensive delicacies. These are then served to gullible tourists, who will eat anything they can't pronounce."

—*Chris Harris*

"You are about to have your first experience with a Greek lunch. I will kill you if you pretend to like it."

—*Jacqueline Kennedy Onassis*

"That is no reason to bypass this beautiful country, whose master chefs have a well-deserved worldwide reputation for trying to trick people into eating snails. Nobody is sure how this got started. Probably a couple of French master chefs were standing around one day, and they found a snail, and one of them said: 'I bet that if we called this something like "escargot," tourists would eat it.' Then they had a hearty laugh, because 'escargot' is the French word for 'fat crawling bag of phlegm.'"

—*Dave Barry,* Dave Barry's Only Travel
Guide You'll Ever Need, *1991*

"The South excelled in two things which the French deem essential to civilization: a code of manners and a native cuisine."

—*John Peale Bishop*

"When helicopters were snatching people from the grounds of the American embassy compound during the panic of the final Vietcong push into Saigon, I was sitting in the front of the television set shouting, 'Get the chefs! Get the chefs!'"

—*Calvin Trillin*

"Only a rank degenerate would drive 1,500 miles across Texas without eating a chicken fried steak."

—*Larry McMurtry,* In a Narrow Grave: Essays on Texas, *1968*

"The problem with eating Italian food is that five or six days later you're hungry again."

—*George Miller*

"It takes some skill to spoil a breakfast—even the English can't do it."

—*John Kenneth Galbraith*

"When the taste changes with every bite and the last bite is as good as the first, that's Cajun."

—*Paul Prudhomme*

"Italy is like cooked macaroni —
yards and yards of soft tenderness,
raveled round everything."

—D. H. Lawrence

"I don't want to be in the same country as goat cheese. It always tastes the way a yak looks in one of those National Geographic specials."

—*Erma Bombeck*

"If there is anything we Chinese are serious about, it is neither religion or learning, but food."

—*Lin Yutang*

"Pâté: A French meatloaf that has had a couple of cocktails."

—*Carol Cutler*

"A favorite dish in Kansas is creamed corn on a stick."

—*Jeff Harms*

"People ask me all the time about the secret to good New Orleans cooking. The secret—ta da!—is in the seasoning."

—*Emeril Lagasse,* Emeril's New New Orleans Cooking, *1993*

"The food in Yugoslavia is either very good or very bad. One day they served us fried chains."

—*Mel Brooks*

"Americans are just beginning to regard food the way the French always have. Dinner is not what you do in the evening before something else. Dinner is the evening."

—*Art Buchwald*

"I had the new Chinese-German food recently. It tastes great, but an hour later you're hungry for POWER!"

—*Ron Ellis*

"Cantonese will eat anything in the sky but airplanes, anything in the sea but submarines, and anything with four legs but the table."

—*Amanda Bennet*

"Nachman's Rule: When it comes to foreign food, the less authentic the better."

—*Gerald Nachman*

"Americans will eat garbage, provided you sprinkle it liberally with ketchup, mustard, chili sauce, Tabasco sauce, cayenne pepper, or any other condiment which destroys the original flavor of the dish."

—*Henry Miller*

On Chinese food:
"You do not sew with a fork, and I see no reason why you should eat with knitting needles."

—*Miss Piggy, in* Miss Piggy's Guide to Life
(as Told to Henry Beard), *1981*

"Feasting is also closely related to memory. We eat certain things in a particular way in order to remember who we are. Why else would you eat grits in Madison, New Jersey?"

—*Jeff Smith,* The Frugal Gourmet Keeps the Feast, *1995*

"Believe it or not, Americans eat 75 *acres* of pizza a day."

—*Boyd Matson*

"Bouillabaisse is only good because it is cooked by the French, who if they cared to try, would produce an excellent and nutritious substitute out of cigar stumps and empty matchboxes."

—*Norman Douglas, "Rain on the Hills"*

"In the 20th century, the French managed to get a death grip on the myth that they produce the world's best food. The hype has been carefully orchestrated, and despite the fact that the most popular food in the last quarter has undoubtedly been Italian the French have managed to maintain that mental grip."

—*Clarissa Dickson Wright, Food, 1999*

"Would I prepare the dinner? Why not? Had I any experience in cooking? No. Would I know how to proceed? Why, of course. All Italians can sing. All Italians can cook."

—*Angelo Pellegrini, The Unprejudiced Palate, 1948*

"The food in Yugoslavia is fine if you like pork tartare."

—*Ed Begley Jr.*

"Never eat anything you can't pronounce."

—*Erma Bombeck*

"Billions of people eat with two sticks, including some who don't have to. Nothing suits me more than being in a party of diners at a Chinese restaurant when show-offs ask for chopsticks. They don't use them right—they pick up dainty morsels one at a time and convey them precariously from table to mouth, which is like trying to carry a bowling ball with two tenpins, instead of holding the food bowl up directly under the chin and using the sticks to shovel gobs of food directly into the mouth, the way the Chinese do."

—*Roger Welsch,* Diggin' In and Piggin' Out, *1997*

On lamb couscous:
"A fine festive dish to set in the middle of a well-crowded table. They present the whole sheep on a vast tray in the Middle East, eyes and all. Yum yum."

—*Jennifer Paterson,* The Two Fat Ladies Ride Again, *1997*

"Yes, I'll admit that I was relieved to find that there were still pigeons left in the squares of San Francisco; it occurred to me that since my previous visit, every last one of them might have been snatched up, smoked, and thrown on a bed of radicchio."

—*Calvin Trillin, "My Life in Wine,"*
in the Nation, *April 27, 1985*

"Everything ends this way in France—everything. Weddings, christenings, duels, burials, swindlings, diplomatic affairs—everything is a pretext for a good dinner."

—*Jean Anouilh*

"In England, there are sixty different religions, but only one sauce."

—*Voltaire*

"Southerners don't much like sweetened corn breads, but it's never bothered us Yankees."

—*John Hadamuscin,* John Hadamuscin's
Down Home, *1993*

"The French, gourmets and lovers all, have made a veritable art of culinary seduction."

—*Greg and Beverly Frazier,*
Aphrodisiac Cookery, *1970*

"Romanian-Yiddish cooking has killed more Jews than Hitler."

—*Zero Mostel*

Heaven to Taste

Favorite Dishes

"Oh, God above, if heaven has a taste it must be an egg with butter and salt, and after the egg is there anything in the world lovelier than fresh warm bread and a mug of sweet golden tea?"

—*Frank McCourt,* Angela's Ashes, *1996*

"My idea of heaven is eating *pâtés de foie gras* to the sound of trumpets."

—*Sydney Smith*

"A simple salad can be pure heaven."
—*Emeril Lagasse,* Emeril's New New Orleans Cooking, *1993*

"Tell me what you eat, and I will tell you what you are."
—*Anthelme Brillat-Savarin,* Physiologie du Goût, *1825*

"Chili is not so much food as a state of mind. Addictions to it are formed early in life and the victims never recover. On blue days of October I get this passionate yearning for a bowl of chili, and I nearly lose my mind."

—*Margaret Cousins*

"As everybody knows, there is only one infallible recipe
for the perfect omelette: your own."

—*Elizabeth David*

"There's no better season for pancakes than spring-
time, when the sugar maple is running and fresh syrup
is made."

—*John Hadamuscin,* John Hadamuscin's
Down Home, 1993

"Oysters are more beautiful than any religion. . . .
There's nothing in Christianity or Buddhism that quite
matches the sympathetic unselfishness of an oyster."

—*Saki*

"There are certain dishes that can quietly haunt
your life."

—*John Thorne,* Pot on the Fire, 2000

"Peanut butter—the pâté of childhood."

—*Florence Fabricant*

"It requires a certain kind of mind to see beauty in a hamburger bun."

—*Ray Kroc*

"And the best bread was of my mother's own making—the best in all the land!"

—*Henry James*

"If I could only have one food for the rest of my life? That's easy: Pez. Cherry-flavored Pez."

—*Jerry O'Connell as Vern Tessio,*
in Stand by Me, *1986*

"Mustard's no good without roast beef."

—*Chico Marx, in* Monkey Business, *1931*

"There are many miracles in the world to be celebrated and, for me, garlic is the most deserving."

—*Leo Buscaglia*

"I've long said that if I were about to be executed and were given a choice of my last meal, it would be bacon and eggs. There are few sights that appeal to me more than the streaks of lean and fat in a good side bacon, of the lovely round of pinkish meat framed in delicate white fat that is Canadian bacon frying in the morning, save perhaps the smell of coffee brewing."

—James Beard

"Bring porridge, bring sausage, bring fish for a start,
Bring kidneys and mushrooms and partridges' legs,
But let the foundation be bacon and eggs."

—A. P. Herbert

"My favorite sandwich is peanut butter, baloney, cheddar cheese, lettuce, mayonnaise on toasted bread with catsup on the side."

—Hubert Humphrey

"Peanut butter is mother's milk to me."

—Jack Nicholson

"Chutney is marvelous. I'm mad about it. To me, it's very imperial."

—*Diana Vreeland*

"Roast beef, medium, is not only a food—it is a philosophy."

—*Edna Ferber*

"And the Quangle Wangle said
To himself on the crumpety tree
'Jam and Jelly and bread
are the best of foods for me.'"

—*Edward Lear*

"Many's the long night I've dreamed of cheese—toasted mostly."

—*Robert Louis Stevenson,* Treasure Island, *1883*

"Cheese. The adult form of milk."

—*Richard Condon,* A Talent for Loving, *1961*

"Sausage, in all its forms and flavors, is a supremely festive food—think about the feasts, blasts, BBQs. It can enrich, exult, and shout down tamer fare. Sausage—simmering in its own juices and bursting with flavor—is the very definition of temptation and satiation."

—*Jody Maroni, in Brigit Binn's* Jody Maroni's Sausage Kingdom Cookbook, *1997*

"The green and gold of my delight—
Asparagus with Hollandaise."

—*Thomas Augustine Daly*

"If I go down for anything in history, I would like to be known as the person who convinced the American people that catfish is one of the finest eating fishes in the world."

—*Willard Scott*

"I can't think of anything more down-home than the humble, all-American meat loaf for a casual satisfying supper."

—*John Hadamuscin,* John Hadamuscin's Down Home, *1993*

"The olive tree is surely the richest gift of Heaven."

—Thomas Jefferson

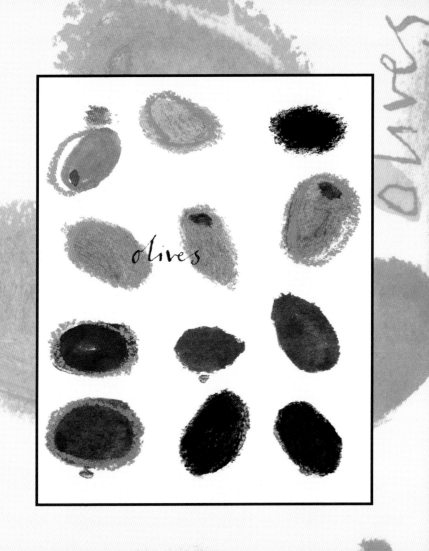

olives

"Oysters are the most tender and delicate of all seafoods. They stay in bed all day and night. They never work or take exercise, are stupendous drinkers, and wait for their meals to come to them."

—*Hector Bolitho*

"Part of the secret of success in life is to eat what you like and let the food fight it out inside."

—*Mark Twain*

"Fish, to taste right, must swim three times—in water, in butter and in wine."

—*Polish proverb*

"Truffles . . . quite possibly the world's sexiest food. You never forget your first one, or stop hungering for your next."

—*Sally Schneider*

"Too few people understand a really good sandwich."

—*James Beard*

"Give me a platter of choice finnan haddie, freshly
cooked in its bath of water and milk, add melted butter,
a slice or two of hot toast, a pot of steaming Darjeeling
tea, and you may tell the butler to dispense with the
caviar, truffles, and nightingales' tongues."

—*Craig Claiborne*

"You may brag about your breakfast
    foods you eat at break of day,
Your crisp delightful shavings and your
    stack of last year's hay,
Your toasted flakes of rye and corn that
    fairly swim in cream,
Or rave about a sawdust mash, an
    epicurean dream.
But none of these appeals to me, though
    all of them I've tried—
The breakfast I liked the best was
    sausage mother fried."

—*Edgar A. Guest, "Sausage,"* Collected Verse, *1934*

"The noblest of all dogs is the hot-dog: it feeds the hand that bites it."

—*Laurence J. Peter*

"What a friend we have in cheeses!
For no food more subtly pleases,
Nor plays so grand a gastronomic part;
Cheese imported—not domestic—
For we all get indigestic
From all the pasteurizer's Kraft and sodden art."

—*William Cole, "What a Friend We Have in Cheeses!"*

". . . When Love is dead
Ambition fled,
And Pleasure, lad, and Pash,
    You'll still enjoy
    A sausage, boy,
A sausage, boy, and mash."

—*A. P. Herbert, "Sausage and Mash"*

"So where did these cravings come from? I concluded it's the baby *ordering in*. Prenatal takeout. Even without ever being in a restaurant, fetuses develop remarkably discerning palates, and they are not shy about demanding what they want. If they get a hankering, they just pick up the umbilical cord and call. 'You know what would taste good right now? A cheeseburger, large fries, and a vanilla shake. And if you could, hurry it up, because I'm supposed to grow a lung in a half hour.'"

—*Paul Reiser,* Babyhood, *1997*

"Everything I like is either illegal,
immoral, or fattening."

—Alexander Woollcott

The More the Merrier

Sherried cheddar or Brie spread with
fresh fruit slices

pale shrimp
zinged with
limes and peppers

Olives in herbs & olive oil

Luscious fruits

herbes
de
provence

Vivid summer
vegetables

Memorable Meals
and Unforgettable Guests

"The more the merrier; the fewer, the better fare."

—*John Palsgrave*

"I had an excellent repast—the best repast possible—which consisted simply of boiled eggs and bread and butter. It was the quality of these simple ingredients that made the occasion memorable."

—*Henry James*

"With good friends . . . and good food on the board, and good wine in the pitcher, we may well ask: When shall we live if not now?"

—*M. F. K. Fisher,* The Art of Eating, *1954*

"This curry was like a performance of Beethoven's Ninth Symphony that I'd once heard played on a player and amplifier built by personnel of the Royal Electrical and Mechanical Engineers, especially the last movement, with everything screaming and banging 'Joy.' It stunned, it made one fear great art. My father could say nothing after the meal."

—*Anthony Burgess*

"These society women never serve chili."

—*Sam Rayburn, on why he avoided parties,
in* Washington Goes to War, *by David Brinkley, 1988*

"Three little ghostesses
Sitting on postesses,
Eating buttered toastesses,
Greasing their fistesses
Up to their wristesses.
Oh, what beastesses,
To make such feastesses!"

—*Nursery rhyme*

"The most remarkable thing about my mother is that for
thirty years she served the family nothing but leftovers.
The original meal has never been found."

—*Calvin Trillin*

"And that reminds me of that wonderful little lamb stew
I had the other night at Chuck Williams'—it was so
wonderful you could cuddle it in your arms."

—*James Beard*

"Spread the table and contention will cease."

—*English proverb*

"I don't know why it is so easy to conjure up these meals—they are recalled almost effortlessly, with fondness and gratitude. . . . I wish that I could be treated, just once more, to Sunday dinner as it was when I was growing up."

—*Martha Stewart, "Remembering Slow-Cooked Sundays," in* Martha Stewart Living

"As a child, my family's menu consisted of two choices: take it, or leave it."

—*Buddy Hackett*

"Strange to see how a good dinner and feasting reconciles everybody."

—*Samuel Pepys,* Diary, *November 9, 1665*

"If you accept a dinner invitation—you have a moral obligation to be amusing."

—*Wallis Simpson, Duchess of Windsor, in* The Windsor Style, *by Suzy Menkes, 1988*

"Any meal may be their last, so it better be a good one."
—*Joseph "Joe Dogs" Iannuzzi,*
The Mafia Cookbook, *1993*

"The wines that one remembers best are not necessarily the finest that one has tasted, and the highest quality may fail to delight so much as some far more humble beverage drunk in more favourable circumstances."
—*H. Warner Allen*

"We dare not trust our wit for making our house pleasant to our friend, so we buy ice cream."
—*Ralph Waldo Emerson*

"Wit is the salt of conversation, not the food."
—*William Hazlitt*

"We should look for someone to eat and drink with before looking for something to eat and drink, for dining alone is leading the life of a lion or a wolf."
—*Epicurus*

"He hath eaten me out of house and home."
—*William Shakespeare,* Henry IV, Part II, *1598*

"Cold soup is a very tricky thing and it is the rare hostess who can carry it off. More often than not the dinner guest is left with the impression that had he only come a little earlier he could have gotten it while it was still hot."
—*Fran Lebowitz*

"A host is like a general: it takes a mishap to reveal his genius."
—*Horace*

"The kitchen, reasonably enough, was the scene of my first gastronomic adventure. I was on all fours. I crawled into the vegetable bin, settled on a giant onion and ate it, skin and all. It must have marked me for life, for I have never ceased to love the hearty flavor of raw onions."
—*James Beard*

"At a dinner party, one should eat wisely but not too well, and talk well but not too wisely."

—*W. Somerset Maugham*

"Though we eat little flesh and drink no wine,
Yet let's be merry; we'll have tea and toast;
Custards for supper, and an endless host
Of syllabubs and jellies and mince-pies,
And other such lady-like luxuries."

—*Percy Bysshe Shelley*

"The sixth hour: when beasts most graze, birds best peck, and men sit down to that nourishment which is called supper."

—*William Shakespeare,* Love's Labour's Lost, 1595

"In England people actually try to be brilliant at breakfast. That is so dreadful of them! Only dull people are brilliant at breakfast."

—*Oscar Wilde,* An Ideal Husband, 1895

"The cocktail party is probably America's greatest contribution to the world of entertaining."

— Martha Stewart

"And we eat until our souls rise up sighing and the most hidden virtues of our wretched humanity are renewed as that blessed soup seeps into our bones, sweeping away with one stroke the fatigue of all the disappointments gathered along the road of life and restoring to us the uncontrollable sensuality of our twenties."

—*Isabel Allende,* Aphrodite: A Memoir of the Senses, *1998*

"The guest is always right—even if we have to throw him out."

—*Charles Ritz, hotelier*

"Happy is said to be the family which can eat onions together. They are, for the time being, separate from the world, and have a harmony of aspiration."

—*Charles Dudley Warner, "Eighteenth Week,"*
My Summer in a Garden, *1871*

"When I was a kid, Friday was the best day of the week. Not only because there was no school the next day, but because Friday was fish and chips day."

—*Emeril Lagasse,* Emeril's New New Orleans Cooking, *1993*

"A crust eaten in peace is better than a banquet partaken in anxiety."

—*Aesop, "The Town Mouse and the Country Mouse"*

"We should be cheering at each meal, anticipating each dinner party, carefully examining each wine bottle, so that, in the end, each meal is seen as a celebration of the fact that God has given us this world along with all of its treasure stores of mushrooms and artichokes and asparagus and pork ribs and lightly smoked salmon."

—*Jeff Smith,* The Frugal Gourmet Keeps the Feast, *1995*

"The ornament of a house is the friends who frequent it."

—*Ralph Waldo Emerson*

"Hors d'oeuvres must be two things at once: delicious and attractive!"

—*Martha Stewart,* Martha Stewart's
Hors d'Oeuvres Handbook, *1999*

"Welcome the coming, speed the parting guest."

—*Alexander Pope's translation of Homer's* Odyssey

"The idea of a dinner party is rather like the idea of a novel. People who have never written novels say: 'Oh, but they're so long and have so many chapters!'"
—*Laurie Colwin,* Home Cooking, *1988*

"A smiling face is half the meal."
—*Latvian proverb*

"Hospitality, *n*. The virtue which induces us to feed and lodge certain persons who are not in need of food and lodging."
—*Ambrose Bierce,* The Devil's Dictionary, *1911*

"What is pleasanter than the tie of host and guest?"
—*Aeschylus*

"The table became the place for the celebration of all pacts, promises, and real intimacy. To be at the table with someone in Biblical times was to be more intimate than being with them in bed! Eating together was the fullest and most important symbol of intimate sharing."
—*Jeff Smith,* The Frugal Gourmet Keeps the Feast, *1995*

"My wife broke our dog of begging at the table—she let him taste it."

—*Pat Cooper*

"It is very poor consolation to be told that a man who has given one a bad dinner, or poor wine, is irreproachable in private life. Even the cardinal virtues cannot atone for half-cold entries."

—*Oscar Wilde,* The Picture of Dorian Gray, *1891*

"Alone. . . and so am I, if a choice must be made between most people I know and myself. This misanthropic attitude is one I am not proud of, but it is firmly there, based on my increasing conviction that sharing food with another human being is an intimate act that should not be indulged in lightly."

—*M. F. K. Fisher, "A Is for Dining Alone,"*
An Alphabet for Gourmets, *1949*

"Fish and visitors stink in three days."

—*Benjamin Franklin,* Poor Richard's Almanac, *1736*

"The glow of the fire is matched by an inner glow from the wine and the fish and we don't say much except murmurs of appreciation."

—*Robert M. Pirsig,* Zen and the Art of Motorcycle Maintenance, *1974*

"I entertained on a cruising trip that was so much fun that I had to sink my yacht to make my guests go home."

—*F. Scott Fitzgerald,* The Last Tycoon, *1941*

Live to Eat

Carrots with dill

Spicy potatoes

The Pleasure of Food

"Man is born to eat."
—*Craig Claiborne,* Craig Claiborne's Kitchen Primer, *1969*

"Eating is touch carried to the bitter end."
—*Samuel Butler*

"Every man should eat and drink, and enjoy the good
of all his labor, it is the gift of God."
—*Ecclesiastes 3:13*

"Give them great meals of beef and iron and steel, they
will act like wolves and fight like devils."
—*William Shakespeare,* Henry V, *1600*

"Almost every person has something secret he likes
to eat."
—*M. F. K. Fisher, "Borderland,"* Serve It Forth, *1937*

"Statistics show that of those who contract the habit
of eating, very few ever survive."
—*Wallace Irwin*

"All people are made alike.
They are made of bones, flesh and dinners.
Only the dinners are different."

—*Gertrude Louise Cheney*

"A true gastronome should always be ready to eat,
just as a soldier should always be ready to fight."

—*Charles Monselet*

"Food has always meant more than feeding. Food is
bonding, sacrament, joy. A quotidian public delight."

—*Sallie Tisdale,* The Best
Thing I Ever Tasted, *2000*

"I won't eat anything that has intelligent life, but I'd
gladly eat a network executive or a politician."

—*Marty Feldman*

"I have never regretted Paradise Lost since I discovered
that it contained no eggs-and-bacon."

—*Dorothy Sayers*

"Dunking is proper for doughnuts; it is barbaric for bagels."

—*William Safire*

"Then, of course, comes the moment during my weekly lunch with the President when he turns to me and utters those historic words, 'You gonna eat that?'"

—*Al Gore*

"I am a great eater of beef, and I believe that does harm to my wit."

—*William Shakespeare,* Twelfth Night, *1602*

"When they ask me what I want, I say, 'What do you think I want? This is America, I want a bowl of red meat. Forget about that! Bring me a live cow over to the table! I'll carve off what I want and ride the rest home.'"

—*Denis Leary,* No Cure for Cancer, *1992*

"Never eat anything whose listed ingredients cover more than one-third of the package."

—*Joseph Leonard*

"I like the philosophy of the sandwich, as it were. It typifies my attitude to life, really. It's all there, it's fun, it looks good, and you don't have to wash up afterwards."

—*Molly Parkin*

"For the millions of us who live glued to computer keyboards at work and TV monitors at home, food may be more than entertainment. It may be the only sensual experience left."

—*Barbara Ehrenreich*

"Breakfast cereals that come in the same colors as polyester leisure suits make oversleeping a virtue."

—*Fran Lebowitz*

"There is more simplicity in the man who eats caviar on impulse than the man who eats Grape-Nuts on principle."

—*G. K. Chesterton*

"Bad men live that they may eat and drink, whereas good men eat and drink that they may live."

—*Socrates*

"There were the cheeses, the *saucissons,* the rabbit and hare and pork *pâté,* the pale scoops of rillettes, the *confits de canard*—it would have been madness not to try them all."

—*Peter Mayle,* Toujours Provence, *1991*

"No man is lonely while eating spaghetti; it requires so much attention."

—*Christopher Morley*

"A good eater must be a good man; for a good eater must have good digestion, and a good digestion depends upon a good conscience."

—*Benjamin Disraeli*

"The whole of nature, as has been said, is a conjugation of the verb to eat, in the active and the passive."

—*William Ralph Inge*

"I will not eat oysters. I want my food dead—not sick, not wounded—dead."

—*Woody Allen*

Live to Eat

"The pig, if I am not mistaken,
Supplies us sausage, ham, and bacon.
Let others say his heart is big—
I call it stupid of the pig."

—Ogden Nash, "The Pig," Happy Days, 1933

"Me, I like to start the day off with a good meal,
something that will stick to my ribs the whole day."

—DJ K-Rock

"I do not like them,
Sam-I-Am.
I do not like
green eggs and ham."

—Dr. Seuss, Green Eggs and Ham, 1960

"She felt so lost and lonely. One chile in walnut sauce
left on the platter after a fancy dinner couldn't feel any
worse than she did."

—Laura Esquivel, Like Water for Chocolate, 1989

"Man is the only animal, I believe,
who pretends he is thinking of other
things when he is eating."

—Robert Lynd

"I come from a family where gravy is considered
a beverage."

—*Erma Bombeck*

"Shake and shake
The catsup bottle,
None will come,
And then a lot'll."

—*Richard Armour*

"This is my clam theory: Eating clams is extremely
sensuous. It's not just cutting something very neatly
with a knife and fork; you're actually picking up the
clam and getting into the shapelessness and the marine
character of it."

—*Camille Paglia*

"Jack Sprat could eat no fat,
His wife could eat no lean.
A real sweet pair of neurotics."

—*Jack Sharkey*

"Il faut manger pour vivre et non pas vivre pour manger."
(One should eat to live, not live to eat.)

—*Molière*, L'Avare, 1668

"According to the statistics, a man eats a prune every
twenty seconds. I don't know who this fellow is, but
I know where to find him."

—*Morey Amsterdam*

"It's been said that fish is a good brain food. That's a
fallacy. But brains are a good fish food."

—*Mel Brooks*

"Little by little, I worked up a list of everything that
according to my own experience and the knowledge
accumulated through centuries in different cultures
enhances passionate life, or just life in general. As is
only natural, food headed the list."

—*Isabel Allende,* Aphrodite: A Memoir
of the Senses, 1998

On airplane food:
"The shiny stuff is tomatoes.
The salad lies in a group.
The curly stuff is potatoes,
The stuff that moves is soup.
Anything that is white is sweet.
Anything that is brown is meat.
Anything that is grey, don't eat."

—*Stephen Sondheim*, *"Do I Hear a Waltz?"* 1965

"At first I paid attention only to taste, storing away the
knowledge that my father preferred salt to sugar and my
mother had a sweet tooth. Later I also began to note
how people ate, and where. My brother liked fancy food
in fine surroundings, my father only cared about the
company, and Mom would eat anything so long as the
location was exotic. I was slowly discovering that if you
watched people as they ate, you could find out who
they were."

—*Ruth Reichl*, Tender at the Bone, 1998

"I believe eating pork makes people stupid."

—*David Steinberg*

"Yuck, this stuff is full of ingredients."

—*Linus, while reading a can label in Charles Schulz's "Peanuts"*

"Ask not what you can do for your country, ask what's for lunch."

—*Orson Welles*

"All real men love to eat."

—*Marlene Dietrich*

"Food, it appeared could be *important*. It could be an event. It had secrets."

—*Anthony Bourdain*, Kitchen Confidential, 2000

"I refuse to spend my life worrying about what I eat. There is no pleasure worth forgoing just for an extra three years in the geriatric ward."

—*John Mortimer*

"To understand the nature of happiness we first have to know what it means to eat one's fill. . . It's not a matter of *how much* you eat, but of the *way* you eat. It's the same with happiness—it doesn't depend on the actual number of blessings we manage to scratch from life, but only our attitudes towards them."

—*Alexander Solzhenitsyn,* The First Circle, 1968

"And ye shall eat the fat of the land."

—*Genesis 45:18*

"I will never eat fish eyeballs, and I do not want to taste anything commonly kept as a house pet."

—*Laurie Colwin,* Home Cooking, 1988

"Fingers were made before forks, and hands before knives."

—*Jonathan Swift,* Polite Conversation, 1738

"My mouth is a happy place."

—*Pat Conroy*

"Did you ever drink kvass made from pears and black-thorn berries? Or vodka infused with raisins and plums? Have you eaten frumenty with milk? My friends, what glorious flavors there are in the world! Once you start eating you can hardly stop."

—*Nikolai Gogol*

"Resist eating anything that when dropped on the floor excites a dog."

—*Erma Bombeck*

"We could not lead a pleasant life,
And 'twould be finished soon,
If peas were eaten with a knife,
And gravy with a spoon.
Eat slowly: only men in rags
And gluttons old in sin
Mistake themselves for carpet bags
And tumble victuals in."

—*Sir Walter Raleigh, "Stans Puer ad Mensam,"*
Laughter from a Cloud, *1923*

"If you can mock a leek, you can eat a leek."

—*William Shakespeare,* Henry V, *1599*

"Whoever is of merry heart has a continual feast."

—*Proverbs 15:15*

"And I have long believed that good food, good eating is all about risk. Whether we're talking about unpasteurized Stilton, raw oysters or working for organized crime 'associates,' food, for me, has always been an adventure."

—*Anthony Bourdain,* Kitchen Confidential, *2000*

"Isn't there any other part of the matzo you can eat?"

—*Marilyn Monroe, after being served matzo ball soup for three meals in a row*

"The two biggest sellers in any bookstore are the cookbooks and the diet books. The cookbooks tell you how to prepare the food and the diet book tells you how not to eat any of it."

—*Andy Rooney*

"I've run more risk eating my way across the country than in all my driving."

—*Duncan Hines*

"He was a bold man that first ate an oyster."

—*Jonathan Swift*

"I believe in compulsory cannibalism. If people were forced to eat what they kill, there would be no more war."

—*Abbie Hoffman,* Revolution for the Hell of It, *1968*

"A professor said, 'People are not interested in freedom but in ham and eggs.' To which I retorted, 'Ten years in prison with only ham and eggs for breakfast would cure that.'"

—*Salvador de Madariaga, on the BBC TV program* Viewpoint, *October 14, 1969*

"Preach not to others what they should eat, but eat as becomes you and be silent."

—*Epictetus*

"Great eaters and great sleepers are incapable of anything else that is great."

—*Henry IV of France*

"Thought depends absolutely on the stomach, but in spite of that, those who have the best stomachs are not the best thinkers."

—*Voltaire*

The Well-Provisioned Table

Divine Dining
and Restaurant Repasts

"Life, within doors, has few pleasanter prospects than a neatly arranged and well-provisioned breakfast table."

—*Nathaniel Hawthorne*, The House of
the Seven Gables, *1851*

"On the table spread the cloth,
Let the knives be sharp and clean,
pickles get and salad both,
Let them each be fresh and green.
With small beer, good ale and wine,
Oh ye gods! how I shall dine."

—*Jonathan Swift*

"A man seldom thinks with more earnestness of anything than he does of his dinner."

—*Samuel Johnson, in* Anecdotes of Samuel Johnson,
by Hester Lynch Piozzi, 1786

"You can't build a meal on a lake."

—*Elsie de Wolfe, objecting to soup as a first course,
in* Elsie de Wolfe, *edited by Jane S. Smith, 1982*

"Diner food is much the same wherever you go—
which is to say, not very good. . . . Going to diners is
not about eating; it's about saving a crucial part of
America's heritage."

—*Bill Bryson,* I'm a Stranger Here Myself, 1999

"That all-softening, overpowering knell,
The Tocsin of the Soul—the dinner-bell."

—*George Gordon, Lord Byron,* Don Juan (1821)

"Do you know on this one block you can buy croissants
in five different places? There's one store called Bonjour
Croissant. It makes me want to go to Paris and open up
a store called Hello Toast."

—*Fran Lebowitz*

"Routine in cuisine is a crime."

—*Édouard Nignon*

"Manhattan is a narrow island off the coast of New
Jersey devoted to the pursuit of lunch."

—*Raymond Sokolov*

"The wide intervals of the bill [of fare] were packed with dishes calculated to insult a cannibal."

—*Mark Twain, about a displeasing menu,*
"At the Appetite Cure," 1898

"Conversation is the enemy of good wine and food."

—*Alfred Hitchcock*

"Dining is and always was a great artistic opportunity."

—*Frank Lloyd Wright*

"Women alone always order sole. It means something."

—*John Dos Passos,* Most Likely to Succeed, 1954

"I'll have whichever is pink and doesn't smell like the bottom of a gym bag."

—*Bill Bryson, on ordering salad dressing in restaurants,*
I'm a Stranger Here Myself, 1999

"Criticizing someone's favorite neighborhood Chinese restaurant is like criticizing their children. They can. You can't."

—*Arthur Schwartz*

"There's an old joke. Uh, two elderly women are at a Catskills mountain resort, and one of 'em says, 'Boy, the food in this place is really terrible.' The other one says, 'Yeah, I know, and such small portions.' Well, that's essentially how I feel about life."

—*Woody Allen as Alvy Singer in* Annie Hall, *1977*

"The guests can wait for dinner, but my chef doesn't wait for the guests."

—*Wallis Simpson, Duchess of Windsor, in*
The Windsor Style, *by Suzy Menkes, 1988*

"All human history attests
That happiness for a man—the hungry sinner!—
Since Eve ate apples, much depends on dinner."

—*George Gordon, Lord Byron*

"A man is in general better pleased when he has a good dinner upon his table, than when his wife talks Greek."

—*Samuel Johnson, in* Johnsonian Miscellanies,
edited by George Birkbeck Hill, 1897

"Not long ago, there was a fad in certain New York restaurants for the guaranteed thirty-minute lunch. . . . If that isn't a recipe for tension and indigestion, I'll swallow my cell phone."
—*Peter Mayle,* Encore Provence, *1999*

"I hate people who are not serious about their meals."
—*Oscar Wilde*

"One cannot think well, love well, sleep well, if one has not dined well."
—*Virginia Woolf,* A Room of One's Own, *1929*

"By insisting on having your bottle pointing to the north when your cork is being drawn, and calling the waiter Max, you may induce an impression on your guests which hours of laboured boasting might be powerless to achieve. For this purpose, however, the guests must be chosen as carefully as the wine."
—*Saki, "The Chaplet," 1911*

"The best number for a dinner party is two—myself and a dam' good headwaiter."

—*Nubar Gulbenkian*

"The larger the pepper mill, the lousier the food."

—*Mike Kalina*

"We went down a few steps and found antipasti winking and glistening on the table in the front, as beautiful as jewelry. There were eggplants the color of amethysts and plates of sliced salami and bresaola that looked like stacks of rose petals left to dry. Roasted tomatoes burst invitingly apart and red peppers were plump and slicked with oil."

—*Ruth Reichl,* Tender at the Bone, 1998

"The food here is so tasteless you could eat a meal of it and belch and it wouldn't remind you of anything."

—*Redd Foxx*

"Show me another pleasure like dinner,
which comes every day and lasts an hour."

— Charles-Maurice de
Talleyrand-Périgord

"I never eat in a restaurant that's over a hundred feet off the ground and won't stand still."

—*Calvin Trillin*

"At fast-food restaurants, you never run the risk of finding peas on your plate. You don't even get a plate."

—*Dave Barry,* Dave Barry's Bad Habits, *1987*

"Try the Andy Warhol New York City Diet: when I order in a restaurant, I order everything I don't want, so I have a lot to play around with while everyone else eats."

—*Andy Warhol, "Beauty,"* The Philosophy of Andy Warhol: From A to B and Back Again, *1975*

"He has seen the future and it is hamburgers."

—*David Halberstam, on Ray Kroc's decision to buy and expand the original McDonald's,* The Fifties, *1993*

"There's a pizza place near where I live that sells only slices. In the back, you can see a guy tossing a triangle in the air."

—*Steven Wright*

"Let's take food as we have found it. It is more than possible that the cities we have passed through, traffic-harried, there are good and distinguished restaurants with menus of delight. But in the eating places along the roads the food has been clean, tasteless, colorless, and of a complete sameness. It is almost as though the customers had no interest in what they ate as long as it had no character to embarrass them."

—*John Steinbeck,* Travels with Charley:
In Search of America, 1962

"The closest these kids come today to civil disobedience is making dinner reservations and not showing up."

—*Bill Maher,* Does Anybody Have
a Problem with That? 1996

"Gastronomical perfection can be reached in these combinations: one person dining alone, unusually upon a couch or a hillside; two persons, of no matter what sex or age, dining in a good restaurant; six people of no matter what sex or age, dining in a good home."

—*M. F. K. Fisher*

"Perhaps most important is to follow your instincts and always pick peasant food. Look at it this way: aristocrats eat mostly to impress other people's peasants."

—*Roger Welsch,* Diggin' In and Piggin' Out, *1997*

"You can find your way across the country using burger joints the way a navigator uses stars."

—*Charles Kuralt*

"What symbolizes the call to privatude, independence, freedom of choice, variety, better than the Swanson TV dinner?"

—*Jeff Smith,* The Frugal Gourmet Keeps the Feast, *1995*

"Great restaurants are, of course, nothing but brothels. There is no point in going to them if one intends to keep one's belt buckled."

—*Frederic Raphael,* Sunday Times
Magazine, *September 25, 1977*

"Is it progress if a cannibal uses knife and fork?"

—*Stanislaw Lec,* Unkempt Thoughts, *1962*

"I don't know why she bothers because, apart from being much too complicated to take in, none of the dishes sounds like anything you want to eat anyway, except maybe on a bet after drinking way too much."

—Bill Bryson, *regarding dinner specials at restaurants,*
I'm a Stranger Here Myself, *1999*

"A dinner invitation, once accepted, is a sacred obligation. If you die before the dinner takes place, your executor must attend."

—*Ward McAllister*

"The key to a successful restaurant is dressing girls in degrading clothes."

—*Michael O'Donoghue*

"Beauty is in the eyes and the mind of the eater. Even if the salmon has been dropped on the linoleum, it comes up smiling. Let the guests remain in equally smiling ignorance."

—*Madeleine Bingham*

"Avoid restaurants with names that are improbable descriptions, such as the Purple Goose, the Blue Kangaroo or the Quilted Orangutan."

—*Calvin Trillin*

"He ordered as one to the menu born."

—*O. Henry*

"Nothing is less important than which fork you use."

—*Emily Post*

"I went to a restaurant. It said 'Breakfast anytime,' So I ordered French toast during the Renaissance."

—*Steven Wright*

"If you can get nothing better out of the world, get a good dinner out of it, at least."

—*Herman Melville,* Moby-Dick, *1851*

"Today's restaurant is theater on a grand scale."

—*Marian Burros*

"Food eaten at a table is better for you than food eaten hunched over a desk, at a counter, or driving in a car. And I believe that, wherever you do it, hurried eating has ruined more digestive systems than *foie gras*."
—*Peter Mayle,* Encore Provence, *1999*

"Eating in places with live plants in their windows is always good. Restaurants with peppermills the size of fire extinguishers and big red menus with the entries spelled with *f*'s instead of *s*'s are always expensive. Italian restaurants with more than 120 entrees are always disappointing. There are no good French restaurants in states which have a *K* in their names. (New Yorque is the exception that proves the rule, whatever that means.)"
—*Miss Piggy, in* Miss Piggy's Guide to Life
(as Told to Henry Beard), *1981*

"Good manners: The noise you don't make when you're eating soup."
—*Bennett Cerf*

"I asked our patient British waiter what this delightfully cool, tasty liquid was. 'Vichyssoise,' came the reply, a word that to this day—even though it's now a tired old warhorse of a menu selection and one I've prepared thousands of times—still has a magical ring to it. I remember everything about the experience: the way our waiter ladled it from a silver tureen into my bowl, the crunch of tiny chopped chives he spooned on as garnish, the rich, creamy taste of leek and potato, the pleasurable shock, the surprise that it was cold."

—*Anthony Bourdain,* Kitchen Confidential, 2000

"Anybody who doesn't think that the best hamburger place in the world is in his hometown is a sissy."

—*Calvin Trillin*

I'll Drink to That

Thirst Quenchers from
Coffee to Champagne

"'I think this calls for a drink' has long been one of our national slogans."

—*James Thurber, "Merry Christmas,"*
Alarms and Diversions, 1957

"Nothing ever tasted better than a cold beer on a beautiful afternoon with nothing to look forward to but more of the same."

—*Hugh Hood*

"Come quickly, I am tasting the stars!"

—*Dom Pérignon, upon discovering champagne*

"There comes a time in every woman's life when the only thing that helps is a glass of champagne."

—*Bette Davis as Katherine "Kit" Marlowe
in* Old Acquaintance, 1943

"Champagne's funny stuff. I'm used to whiskey. Whiskey is a slap on the back, and champagne's a heavy mist before my eyes."

—*James Stewart as Mike Connor in*
The Philadelphia Story, 1940

"To expect to drink decent wine regularly, you must have a good memory, more than a little canniness, a willingness to spend lots of money, and even then, a bit of luck."

—*John Thorne,* Pot on the Fire, *2000*

"Coffee:
Black as the devil,
Hot as hell,
Pure as an angel,
Sweet as love."

—*Charles-Maurice de Talleyrand-Périgord*

"Why don't you get out of that wet coat and into a dry martini?"

—*Robert Benchley as Mr. Osborne in*
The Major and the Minor, *1942*

"God made only water, but man made wine."

—*Victor Hugo, "La Fête chez Thérèse,"*
Les Contemplations, *1856*

"I drink to the general joy of the whole table."

—*William Shakespeare,* Macbeth, *1606*

"Bronze is the mirror of the form; wine, of the heart."

—*Aeschylus,* Fragments

"If you can hold it on your tongue without blowing your ears off, it meets the test."

—*Bill Samuels Jr., on greatness in bourbon, in* Connoisseur, *July 1991*

"Only Irish coffee provides in a single glass all four essential food groups: alcohol, caffeine, sugar, and fat."

—*Alex Levine*

"Once, during Prohibition, I was forced to live for days on nothing but food and water."

—*W. C. Fields*

"The cow is of the bovine ilk;
One end is moo, the other Milk."

—*Ogden Nash*

"Vienna coffee! . . . that sumptuous coffee-house coffee, compared with which all other European and all American hotel is merely fluid poverty."

—*Mark Twain, "At the Appetite Cure," 1898*

"It is only the first bottle that is expensive."

—*French proverb*

"Winemaking is the world's second-oldest profession and, no doubt, it has eased the burden of the world's oldest."

—*Tony Aspler, in the* Toronto Star, *September 21, 1985*

"The fine wine leaves you with something pleasant; the ordinary wine just leaves."

—*Maynard Amerine, in* The New Joys of Wine, *by Clifton Fadiman, 1990*

"Oh the joy of lingering over port and brandy with men in red coats telling dirty stories while it snows outside."

—*Cyril Connolly, on the hour after the fox hunt,* Cyril Connolly: Journals and Memoirs, *1984*

"Religions change; beer and wine remain."
                    —*Hervey Allen,* Anthony Adverse, *1933*

"The coffee was smooth and satisfying, a single gulp of pure caffeine that lingered on the palate and reverberated behind the eyes. I felt lightheaded."
                    —*Ruth Reichl,* Tender at the Bone, *1998*

"Drink no longer water, but use a little wine for thy stomach's sake and thine often infirmities."
                    —*1 Timothy 5:23*

"Drinking when we are not thirsty and making love at any time, Madame—that is all there is to distinguish us from the animals."
                    —*Pierre-Augustin de Beaumarchais*

"'Yes, that's it,' said the Hatter with a sigh: 'it's always tea-time, and we've no time to wash the things between whiles.'"
                    —*Lewis Carroll,* Alice's Adventures in Wonderland, *1865*

"What's the point of non-alcoholic beer? This must be for people who *don't* want to get drunk, but *do* want to spend the entire evening in the bathroom peeing their brains out!"

—*Marsha Doble*

"I have very poor and unhappy brains for drinking; I could well wish courtesy would invent some other custom of entertainment."

—*William Shakespeare*, Othello, 1605

"At one with the One, it didn't mean a thing besides a glass of Guinness on a sunny day."

—*Graham Greene*, Brighton Rock, 1938

"When one comes to think of it, it's odd that there should be so much admiration for prowess in drinking, which after all is merely a domestic virtue."

—*Sir Wilfred Grenfell*

"Bacchus has drowned more men than Neptune."

—*Giuseppe Garibaldi*

"The smell of coffee cooking was a reason for growing up, because children were never allowed to have it and nothing haunted the nostrils all the way out to the barn as did the aroma of boiling coffee."

—*Edna Lewis*

"Man, being reasonable, must get drunk;
The best of Life is but intoxication."

—*George Gordon, Lord Byron*

"My stomach whispered lunch and to hell with time.
I went to look for the liquid moral support of more coffee."

—*Peter Mayle,* Toujours Provence, *1991*

"Although it is better to hide our ignorance, this is hard to do when we relax over wine."

—*Heracleitus*

"I like liquor—its taste and its effects—and that is just the reason why I never drink it."

—*Thomas Stonewall Jackson*

"Temperance is the control of all the functions of our bodies. The man who refuses liquor, goes in for apple pie and develops a paunch, is no ethical leader for me."
—*John Erskine*

"Eat bread at pleasure, drink wine by measure."
—*Randle Cotgrave*

"Boys should abstain from all uses of wine until their eighteenth year, for it is wrong to add fire to fire."
—*Plato*

"Wine is sunlight, held together by water."
—*Galileo*

"Of all the unchristian beverages that ever passed my lips, Turkish coffee is the worst."
—*Mark Twain,* Innocents Abroad, 1869

"The whole world is about three drinks behind."
—*Humphrey Bogart*

"Wine is only sweet to happy men."

—*John Keats*

"In Mexico, we have a word for sushi: bait."

—*José Simon*

"When there is plenty of wine, sorry and worry take wing."

—*Ovid*

"Drunkenness is simply voluntary insanity."

—*Seneca*

"I am prepared to believe that a dry martini slightly impairs the palate, but think what it does for the soul."

—*Alec Waugh*

"A woman drove me to drink and I never even had the courtesy to thank her."

—*W. C. Fields*

"You can't drown yourself in drink. I've tried: you float."

—*John Barrymore*

"It provokes the desire, but it takes away the performance. Therefore much drink may be said to be an equivocator with lechery."

—*William Shakespeare*, Macbeth, *1606*

"Even the most naive schoolboy, out on his first date, is well aware of the seductive atmosphere of candlelight and wine."

—*Greg and Beverly Frazier*, Aphrodisiac Cookery, *1970*

"I've made it a rule never to drink by daylight and never to refuse a drink after dark."

—*H. L. Mencken*, New York Post, *September 18, 1945*

"Candy
Is dandy
But liquor
Is quicker."

—*Ogden Nash, "Reflections on Ice-Breaking,"* Hard Lines, *1931*

"I like my convictions undiluted, same as I do my bourbon."

—*George Brent in* Jezebel, *1938*

"Wine is bottled poetry."

—Robert Louis Stevenson

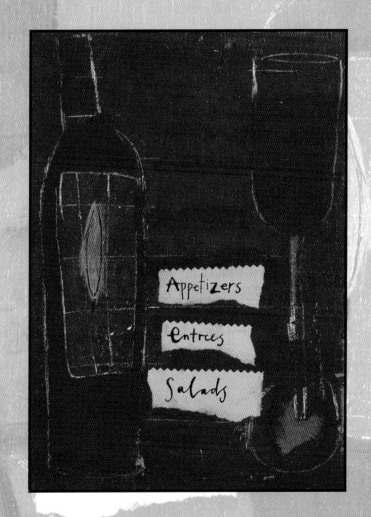

Appetizers

Entrees

Salads

"My grandmother is over eighty and still doesn't need glasses. Drinks right out of the bottle."

—*Henny Youngman*

"I haven't touched a drop of alcohol since the invention of the funnel."

—*Malachy McCourt*

"Most people hate the taste of beer to begin with. It is, however, a prejudice that many people have been able to overcome."

—*Winston Churchill*

"It's a Naive Domestic Burgundy, Without Any Breeding, But I think you'll be Amused by its Presumption."

—*James Thurber, cartoon in*
Men, Women, and Dogs, 1943

"Even though a number of people have tried, no one has yet to find a way to drink for a living."

—*Jean Kerr*

"Good wine is a good familiar creature if it be well used."
—*William Shakespeare*, Othello, *1605*

"I get no kick from champagne.
Mere alcohol doesn't thrill me at all."
—*Cole Porter song, "I Get a Kick out of You,"*
Anything Goes, *1934*

"Wine, *n.* Fermented grape-juice known to the Women's
Christian Union as 'liquor,' sometimes as 'rum.' Wine,
madame, is God's next best gift to man."
—*Ambrose Bierce*, The Devil's Dictionary, *1911*

"I've decided to stop drinking with creeps. I decided to
drink only with friends. I've lost 30 pounds."
—*Ernest Hemingway, in* American Way, *August 1974*

"I don't drink any more—just the same amount."
—*Joe E. Lewis*

"A bottle of wine begs to be shared; I've never met a
miserly wine lover."
—*Clifton Fadiman*

"Champagne, if you are seeking the truth, is better than a lie detector. It encourages a man to be expansive, even reckless, while lie detectors are only a challenge to tell lies successfully."

—*Graham Greene*

"One drink is plenty; two drinks two many, and three not half enough."

—*W. Knox Haynes*

"The morning cup of coffee has an exhilaration about it which the cheering influence of the afternoon or evening cup of tea cannot be expected to reproduce."

—*Oliver Wendell Holmes Sr.*

"Wine that maketh glad the heart of man."

—*Psalms 104:15*

"For me, the most powerful ingredient in *pastis* is not aniseed or alcohol but *ambiance,* and that dictates how and where it should be drunk."

—*Peter Mayle,* Toujours Provence, 1991

"I think if I were a woman I'd wear coffee as a perfume."
—*John Van Druten*

"If all be true that I do think,
There are five reasons we should drink;
Good wine—a friend—or being dry—
Or lest we should be by and by—
Or any other reason why."

—*Henry Aldrich*

"I always keep a supply of stimulant handy in case I see
a snake—which I also keep handy."
—*W. C. Fields*

"One of the disadvantages of wine is that it makes a
man mistake words for thoughts."
—*Samuel Johnson*

On drinking whiskey:
"A torchlight procession marching down your throat."
—*John Louis O'Sullivan*

"*In vino veritas.*" (In wine is truth.)
—*Pliny the Elder,* Historia Naturalis

"A meal without wine is like a day without sunshine."
—*Anthelme Brillat-Savarin*

"There are few hours in life more agreeable than the hour dedicated to the ceremony known as afternoon tea."
—*Henry James*

"Claret is the liquor for boys; port for men; but he who aspires to be a hero must drink brandy."
—*Samuel Johnson, in* The Life of Samuel Johnson, *by James Boswell, 1791*

"Excellent wine generates enthusiasm. And whatever you do with enthusiasm is generally successful."
—*Phillippe de Rothschild*

"If you want to become a rich, pretentious snot—and who doesn't?—you should learn about wine."
—*Dave Barry,* Dave Barry's Bad Habits, *1987*

"The superiority of the article [hot chocolate] both
for health and nourishment will soon give it the same
preference over tea and coffee in America which it
has in Spain."

—*Thomas Jefferson, in a letter to John Adams,*
November 27, 1785

"Wine has a drastic, an astringent taste. I cannot help
wincing as I drink. Ascent of flowers, radiance and heat,
are distilled here to a fiery, yellow liquid. Just behind my
shoulder-blades some dry thing, wide-eyed, gently closes,
gradually lulls itself to sleep. This is rapture. This is relief."

—*Virginia Woolf*

"Cocoa? Cocoa! Damn miserable puny stuff; fit for kittens
and unwashed boys. Did *Shakespeare* drink cocoa?"

—*Shirley Jackson*

"Drink your cocktail as soon as possible. Quickly, while
it's laughing at you."

—*Harry Craddock, author of* The Savoy Hotel
Cocktail Book, *in* GQ, *September 1990*

"A glass of good wine is a gracious creature, and reconciles poor mortality to itself, and that is what few things can do."

—*Sir Walter Scott*

"The only advantage of having lived though the Age of Prohibition is that any liquor tastes good."

—*Don Marquis*

"It was my Uncle George who discovered that alcohol was a food well in advance of modern medical thought."

—*P. G. Wodehouse*, The Inimitable Jeeves, 1924

"Even for those who dislike Champagne . . . there are two Champagnes one can't refuse: Dom Pérignon and the even superior Cristal, which is bottled in a natural-coloured glass that displays its pale blaze, a chilled fire of such prickly dryness that, swallowed, seems not to have been swallowed at all, but instead to have been turned to vapours on the tongue, and burned there to one sweet ash."

—*Truman Capote*

"I am beauty and love;
I am friendship, the comforter;
I am that which forgives and forgets.
The Spirit of Wine."

—*W. E. Henley*

"Burgundy makes you think of silly things; Bordeaux makes you talk about them, and Champagne makes you do them."

—*Anthelme Brillat-Savarin*

"'Oh, for a good cup of tea!' A truly British cry that I echo so often in my travels around four o'clock in the afternoon. Tea is my panacea, my consolation—if you will, my 'fix.'"

—*Diana Kennedy*

"There was no label this time with the words 'DRINK ME' but nevertheless she uncorked it and put it to her lips. 'I know *something* interesting is sure to happen,' she said to herself, 'whenever I eat or drink anything; so I'll just see what this bottle does.'"

—*Lewis Carroll,* Alice's Adventures in Wonderland, *1865*

"The wine they drink in Paradise
They make in Haute Lorraine."

—*G. K. Chesterton, "A Cider Song"*

"When I die I want to decompose in a barrel of porter
and have it served in all the pubs in Dublin. I wonder
would they know it was me?"

—*J. P. Donleavey,* The Ginger Man, *1955*

"The man that isn't jolly after drinking
Is just a driveling idiot, to my thinking."

—*Euripides*

"Brandy is lead in the morning, silver at noon, gold at night."

—*German proverb*

"Champagne and orange juice is a great drink. The
orange improves the champagne. The champagne
definitely improves the orange."

—*Philip, Duke of Edinburgh*

"O thou invisible spirit of wine, if thou hast no name
to be known by, let us call thee devil!"
                    —*William Shakespeare,* Othello, *1605*

"Gazing at the typewriter in moments of desperation,
I console myself with three thoughts: alcohol at six,
dinner at eight, and to be immortal, you've got to be dead."
                    —*Gyles Brandeth*

"Wine makes daily living easier, less hurried, with fewer
tensions and more tolerance."
                    —*Benjamin Franklin*

"Gimme a visky with chincher ale on the side—and
don't be stingy, baby."
                    —*Greta Garbo in* Anna Christie, *1930*

"To taste port is to taste a tiny atom of England and
her past."
                    —*Clifton Fadiman,* Any Number Can Play, *1957*

"Red wine is for children, champagne for men, and brandy for soldiers."

—*Otto von Bismarck*

"If you are cold, tea will warm you—if you are too heated, it will cool you—if you are depressed, it will cheer you— if you are excited, it will calm you."

—*William Gladstone*

"When company comes for dinner, grab a bottle at random and make an elaborate, French-sounding fuss about how you chose it to complement your menu. Say: 'I chose the Escargot '63 rather than the Garçon '72 because the *bonjour* of the *s'il vous plaît* would bring out the *plume de ma tante* of the Cheez Whiz without being too strident for the chili dogs.'"

—*Dave Barry,* Dave Barry's Bad Habits, 1987

"Some years ago, seekers after the gastronomic truth discovered what the French have known for centuries, and pronounced that a little red wine is good for you."

—*Peter Mayle,* Encore Provence, 1999

Garden
of Plenty

Fruit and Vegetable Delights

"What was paradise, but a garden full of vegetables and herbs and pleasure? Nothing there but delights."
—*William Lawson*

"The true Southern watermelon is a boon apart, and not to be mentioned with commoner things. . . . When one has tasted it, he knows what the angels eat. It was not a Southern watermelon that Eve took; we know it because she repented."
—*Mark Twain,* Pudd'nhead Wilson, *1894*

"Talking of Pleasure, this moment I was writing with one hand, and with the other holding to my Mouth a nectarine—how good how fine. It went down all pulpy, slushy, oozy—all its delicious embonpoint melted down my throat like a large, beautified strawberry."
—*John Keats*

"I'm strongs to the finish 'cause I eats me spinach."
—*Popeye, in the cartoon "Popeye," created by Elzie Segar*

"The artichoke above all is a vegetable expression of civilized living, of the long view, of increasing delight by anticipation and crescendo. No wonder it was once regarded as an aphrodisiac. It had no place in the troll's world of instant gratification."

—*Jane Grigson*

"Lettuce is like conversation: it must be fresh and crisp, and so sparkling that you scarcely notice the bitter in it."

—*Charles Dudley Warner*

"The apple is our national fruit, and I like to see that the soil yields it; I judge the country so. The American sun paints himself in these glowing balls amid the green leaves. Man would be more solitary, less friended, less supported, if the land yielded only the useful maize and potato, and withheld this ornamental and social fruit."

—*Ralph Waldo Emerson*, Journals, *1848*

"Genetically altered tomatoes. . . . The FDA says they're perfectly safe. And people with twelve fingers love 'em."

—*Jim Mullen*

"Success to me is like having ten honeydew melons and eating only the top half of each one."

—*Barbra Streisand*

"Melons are the sweet aristocrats of the very large gourd family."

—*Irena Chalmers*

"I stick to asparagus which seems to inspire gentle thought."

—*Charles Lamb*

"We kids feared many things in those days—werewolves, dentists, North Koreans, Sunday School—but they all paled in comparison with Brussels sprouts."

—*Dave Barry,* Dave Barry's Bad Habits, *1987*

"Vegetables are a must on a diet. I suggest carrot cake, zucchini bread, and pumpkin pie."

—Garfield, in the cartoon "Garfield,"
created by Jim Davis

"There are two classes of pears—those that taste like hair-wash and those that do not."

—Edward Bunyard, "The Anatomy of Dessert,"
Country Life, *September 16, 1993*

"Artichoke—the vegetable of which one has more at the finish than the start of a dinner."

—Philip Dormer Stanhope, Lord Chesterfield

"No vegetable exists which is not better slightly undercooked."

—James Beard

"The embarrassing thing is that the salad dressing is out-grossing my films."

—Paul Newman

"There is no dignity in the bean. Corn, with no affectation of superiority, is, however, the child of song. It waves in all literature. But mix it with beans, and its high tone is gone. Succotash is vulgar."

—*Charles Dudley Warner*

"Vegetables are interesting but lack a sense of purpose when unaccompanied by a good cut of meat."

—*Fran Lebowitz*

"Nature alone is antique and the oldest art a mushroom."

—*Thomas Carlyle*

"I don't like spinach, and I'm glad I don't, because if I liked it, I'd eat it, and I just hate it."

—*Clarence Darrow*

"After all the trouble you go to, you get about as much actual 'food' out of eating an artichoke as you would from licking thirty or forty postage stamps."

—*Miss Piggy, in* Miss Piggy's Guide to Life
(as Told to Henry Beard), *1981*

"The beet is the most intense of vegetables. The radish, admittedly, is more feverish, but the fire of the radish is a cold fire, the fire of discontent, not of passion. Tomatoes are lusty enough, yet there runs through tomatoes an undercurrent of frivolity. Beets are deadly serious."

—*Tom Robbins,* Jitterbug Perfume, *1984*

"O precious food! Delight of the mouth!
Oh, much better than gold, masterpiece of Apollo!
O flower of all the fruits! O ravishing melon!"

—*Marc-Antoine Girard, Sieur de Saint-Amant*

About the strawberry:
"Doubtless God could have made a better berry, but doubtless God never did."

—*William Butler*

"There is something eternal about the freshness a lemon imparts. . . . They make you pucker and gnash, but you can't stay mad at lemons for long."

—*Molly O'Neill, on lemons in spring recipes,
in the* New York Times, *July 9, 1995*

"Eating an artichoke is like getting to know someone really well."

—Willi Hastings

artichoke

"Large, naked, raw carrots are acceptable as food only to those who live in hutches eagerly awaiting Easter."

—*Fran Lebowitz*

"Lettuce is divine, although I'm not sure it's really food."

—*Diana Vreeland*

"Cabbage, *n.* A familiar kitchen-garden vegetable about as large and wise as a man's head."

—*Ambrose Bierce,* The Devil's Dictionary, *1911*

"A cucumber should be well sliced, and dressed with pepper and vinegar, and then thrown out as good for nothing."

—*Samuel Johnson, in* Journal of a Tour to
the Hebrides with Samuel Johnson,
by James Boswell, October 5, 1773

"Well brought up English girls are taught . . . to boil veggies for at least a month and a half."

—*Calvin Trillin,* Third Helpings, *1983*

"I tried eating vegetarian. But I felt like a wimp going into a restaurant: 'What do you want to eat, sir?' 'Broccoli.' Hey, broccoli is a side dish, folks, always was, always will be, okay?"

—*Denis Leary,* No Cure for Cancer, *1992*

"An apple is an excellent thing—until you have tried a peach!"

—*George Du Maurier*

"I say it's spinach, and I say the hell with it."

—*E. B. White*

"I do not know of a flowering plant that tastes good and is poisonous. Nature is not out to get you."

—*Euell Gibbons*

"Salsa has now passed ketchup as America's favorite condiment. Isn't that amazing? You know it's bad when even our vegetables are starting to lose their jobs to Mexico."

—*Jay Leno*

On pears:
"I count pears among the most delicious and sensuous of fruits. The sweetness of a perfectly ripe pear is unsurpassed; the round shape and subtle shadings of green, yellow, brown, and rose have made pears a favorite of water colorists and other artists for centuries."
—*Jay Kordich,* The Juiceman's Power of Juicing, *1992*

"On the subject of spinach: Divide into little piles. Rearrange again into new piles. After five or six maneuvers, sit back and say you are full."
—*Delia Ephron*

"I have always loved the mushroom as the symbol of the cleverness of the Creator. After all, mushrooms grow out of the waste and ruin of the cow or horse field. They grow from dead leaves and horse dung! Who else but the Holy One could come up with something as clever as that? Or as delicious?"
—*Jeff Smith,* The Frugal Gourmet Keeps the Feast, *1995*

"Yes, we have no bananas,
We have no bananas today."
>—*Frank Silver and Irving Cohn, "Yes, We Have No Bananas"*

"I do not like broccoli, and I haven't liked it since I was a little boy and my mother made me eat it. And I'm President of the United States, and I'm not going to eat any more broccoli!"
>—*George Bush, on the menus aboard Air Force One,
>in the* New York Times, *March 23, 1990*

"Avoid fruits and nuts. You are what you eat."
>—*Garfield, in the cartoon "Garfield," created by Jim Davis*

"Rolf came up and put a morel into my mouth. It had an earthy flavor, like the entire countryside concentrated into a single bite."
>—*Ruth Reichl,* Tender at the Bone, *1998*

"The cherry tomato is a marvelous invention, producing as it does a satisfactorily explosive squish when bitten."
>—*Miss Manners (Judith Martin)*

"There are some things that sound too funny to eat—guacamole. That sounds like something you yell when you're on fire."

—*George Carlin*

"Do you hunt your own truffles or do you hire a pig?"

—*Jean McClatchy's suggestion for an icebreaker*

"A salad should never be just a dish of greens. Every salad should sparkle with flavor, cleanse the palate, and beef up the appetite."

—*Emeril Lagasse,* Emeril's New New Orleans Cooking, *1993*

"Presently we were aware of an odour gradually coming towards us, something musky, fiery, savoury, mysterious—a hot, drowsy smell, that lulls the senses and yet enflames them—the truffles were coming."

—*William Makepeace Thackeray*

"I'm not a vegetarian because I love animals; I'm a vegetarian because I hate plants."

—*A. Whitney Brown*

On apricots:
"A Persian poet called these luscious fruits the seeds of the sun, and one bite of the small golden orbs explains why."

—*Jay Kordich,* The Juiceman's Power of Juicing, *1992*

"Iceberg lettuce is perhaps the most aptly named plant in the world, and should be avoided as though you were the *Titanic* with a second chance."

—*Alan Koehler*

"As one of the kids rummaged in the refrigerator, he said, 'What's this?'

"'It's celery and it's good for you.' He said, 'If it's so great, then how come it never danced on television?'

"I couldn't answer him."

—*Erma Bombeck,* Family—the Ties
That Bind . . . and Gag! *1987*

"There's someone at every party who eats all the celery."
—*Kin Hubbard*

"I have no religious or moral objection to vegetables but they are, as it were, dull. They are the also-rans of the plate. One takes an egg, or a piece of meat, or fish, with pleasure but then one has, as a kind of penance, to dilute one's pleasure with a damp lump of boskage."
—*Frank Muir,* You Can't Have Your Kayak and Heat It, *1973*

"All millionaires love a baked apple."
—*Ronald Firbank,* Vainglory, *1925*

"I never worry about diets. The only carrots that interest me are the number you get in a diamond."
—*Mae West*

"A salad is not a meal. It is a style."
—*Fran Lebowitz,* Metropolitan Life, *1974*

"Life ovaled
a goblet to contain
its clarity, its darkness,
its coolness.
O kiss
of the lips
on the fruit
teeth
and lips
dripping
a fragrant amber,
the liquid
light of the plum!"

—*Pablo Neruda, from "Ode to the Plum"*

"Training is everything. . . . Cauliflower is nothing but
a cabbage with a college education."

—*Mark Twain,* Pudd'nhead Wilson, *1894*

"It is said that the effect of eating too much lettuce is soporific."

— Beatrix Potter, THE TALE OF
THE FLOPSY BUNNIES, 1909

Devil's Food

Cake and Other Sweet Treats

"That year I discovered the secret of every experienced cook: desserts are a cheap trick. People love them even when they're bad. And so I began to bake, appreciating the alchemy that can turn flour, water, chocolate, and butter into devil's food cake and make it disappear in a flash."

—*Ruth Reichl,* Tender at the Bone, *1998*

"A whole fleet of Rolls Royces would not have compensated for the home-made fresh plum ice cream which disappeared from our tree."

—*Waverly Root*

"The sweets I remember best were white and tubular, much thinner than any cigarette, filled with a dark chocolate filling. If I found one now I am sure it would have the taste of hope."

—*Graham Greene*

"Life is like a box of chocolates. You never know what you're going to get."

—*Tom Hanks in* Forrest Gump, *1994*

"A dessert without cheese is like a beautiful woman with only one eye."

—*Anthelme Brillat-Savarin*

"Dessert should close the meal gently and not in a pyrotechnic blaze of glory. No cultivated feeder, already well-fed, thanks his host for confronting him with a dessert so elaborate that not to eat it is simply rude—like refusing to watch one's host blow up Bloomingdale's."

—*Alan Koehler*

"Why do you eat that stuff? There's no food in your food."

—*Joan Cusack as Constance Dobbler in* Say Anything, *1989*

"The Queen of Hearts, she made some tarts,
All on a summer day:
The Knave of Hearts, he stole those tarts
And took them quite away!"

—*Nursery rhyme in Lewis Carroll's* Alice's Adventures in Wonderland, *1865*

"Why is birthday cake the only food you can blow out and spit on and everybody wants to get a piece?"
—*Bobby Keller*

"You can tell a lot about a fellow's character by his way of eating jelly beans."
—*Ronald Reagan*

"Chocolate: It flatters you for a while, it warms you for an instant; then all of a sudden, it kindles a mortal fever in you."
—*Marquise Marie de Sévigné*

"Health food may be good for the conscience, but Oreos taste a hell of a lot better."
—*Robert Redford*

"I doubt whether the world holds for anyone a more soul-stirring surprise than the first adventure with ice-cream."
—*Heywood Broun, "Holding a Baby,"* Seeing Things at Night, *1921*

"The only reason for being a bee that I know of is making honey . . . and the only reason for making honey is so I can eat it."

—*Winnie-the-Pooh, created by A. A. Milne*

"Kids don't want to eat wholesome foods: kids want to eat grease and sugar. This is why, given the choice, kids will eat things that do not qualify as food at all, such as Cheez Doodles, Yoo-Hoo, Good & Plenty, and those little wax bottles that contain colored syrup with enough sugar per bottle to dissolve a bulldozer in two hours."

—*Dave Barry,* Dave Barry's Bad Habits, 1987

"Dinner is to a day what dessert is to dinner."

—*Michael Dorris, "The Quest for Pie,"*
Paper Trail, 1994

"There is something in the red of a raspberry pie that looks as good to a man as the red in a sheep looks good to a wolf."

—*Edgar Watson Howe,* Sinner Sermons, 1926

"Fancy is as fancy does, and nothing could be fancier than little fruit tartlets."

—Jennifer Paterson,
THE TWO FAT LADIES
RIDE AGAIN, 1997

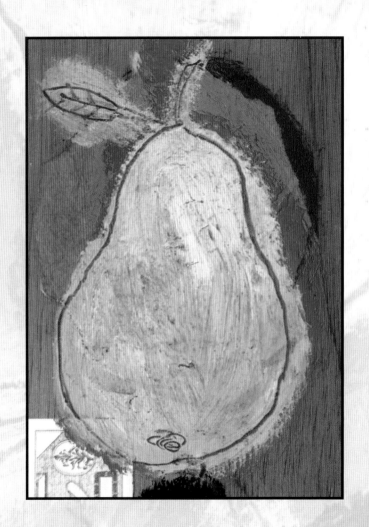

"Promises and pie-crusts are made to be broken."

—*Jonathan Swift*

"A *tarte au citron,* a dessert to die for or, given its butterfat content, to die from."

—*Michael Mewshaw, on Parisian pastries, in the* New York Times, *March 3, 1991*

"I've spent half a century jousting with the demons of flesh and chocolate."

—*Isabel Allende,* Aphrodite: A Memoir of the Senses, *1998*

"The last taste of sweets is sweetest last."

—*William Shakespeare,* Richard II, *1596*

"The most dangerous food is wedding cake."

—*American proverb*

"I want a little sugar in my bowl
I want a little sweetness down in my soul."

—*Nina Simone,* "I Want a Little Sugar in My Bowl"

On eating like a child:
"Chocolate chip cookies: half-sit, half-lie on the bed,
propped up by a pillow. Read a book. Place cookies
next to you on the sheet so that crumbs get in the bed.
As you eat the cookies, remove each chocolate chip
and place it on your stomach. When all the cookies
are consumed, eat the chips one by one, allowing two
per page."

—*Delia Ephron, in the* New York Times, *1983*

"I adore seafood, especially saltwater taffy."

—*Milton Berle*

"The taste of sweetness, whereof a little
More than a little is by much too much."

—*William Shakespeare,* Henry IV, Part I, *1597*

"I prefer Hostess fruit pies to pop-up toaster tarts
because they don't require so much cooking."

—*Carrie Snow*

"'Yes,' said Frog, reaching for a cookie, 'we need will power.'

"'What is will power?' asked Toad.

"'Will power is trying hard *not* to do something you really want to do,' said Frog.

"'You mean like trying *not* to eat all of these cookies?' asked Toad.

"'Right,' said Frog."
— *Arnold Lobel,* The Adventures of Frog and Toad, *1972*

"As one who has achieved the symmetry of a Humphrey Bogart and the grace of a jaguar purely on pastry, I have no truck with lettuce, cabbage and similar chlorophyll. Any dietician will tell you that a running foot of apple strudel contains four times the vitamins of a bushel of beans."
— *S. J. Perelman,* The Most of S. J. Perelman, *1958*

"Why am I bothering to eat this chocolate? I might as well just apply it directly to my thighs."
— *Rhoda Morgenstern, on* The Mary Tyler Moore Show

"My advice to you is not to inquire why or whither, but just enjoy your ice cream while it's on your plate."
—*Thornton Wilder*

"There's hardly anyone whose favorite dessert isn't ice cream in one form or another, especially in the summer."
—*John Hadamuscin,* John Hadamuscin's Down Home, *1993*

"A surfeit of the sweetest things
The deepest loathing to the stomach brings."
—*William Shakespeare,* A Midsummer Night's Dream, *1596*

"If you want to make an apple pie from scratch, you must first create the universe."
—*Carl Sagan*

"An anthology is like all the plums and orange peels picked out of a cake."
—*Sir Walter Raleigh, in a letter to Mrs. Robert Bridges, January 15, 1915*

"For me, it's all about the unerotic possibilities of chocolate. When there's no opportunity for anything erotic, a handful of Hershey's kisses is the next best thing."

—*Peter Gallagher*

"Look, I'm living testament to the great erotic possibilities of chocolate. My parents conceived me after a wonderful meal—and I'd suspect yours did, too!"

—*Alfred Molina, at the movie premier of* Chocolat, *December 4, 2000*

"Good apple pies are a considerable part of our domestic happiness."

—*Jane Austen*

"What is a roofless cathedral compared to a well-built pie?"

—*William Maginn*

The *Passionate Kitchen*

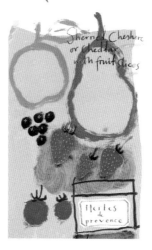

Food and Love

"When I write of hunger, I am really writing about love and the hunger for it, and . . . warmth and the love of it . . . and it is all one."

—*M. F. K. Fisher*

"The most indispensable ingredient of all good home cooking: love for those you are cooking for."

—*Sophia Loren*

"The idea that a potato in the dining room can lead to a frolic in the bedroom is not as ridiculous as it sounds."

—*Greg and Beverly Frazier,* Aphrodisiac Cookery, *1970*

"A loaf of bread,
A jug of wine
And thou, beneath the bough,
Were paradise enow."

—*Omar Khayyám,* Rubaiyat, *eleventh century*

"My idea of heaven is a great big baked potato and someone to share it with."

—*Oprah Winfrey*

"When nobody eats the last chile on the plate, it's usually because none of them wants to look like a glutton, so even though they'd really like to devour it, they don't have the nerve to take it. It was as if they were rejecting a stuffed pepper, which contains every imaginable flavor; sweet as candied citron, juicy as a pomegranate, with the bit of pepper and the subtlety of walnuts, that marvelous chile in walnut sauce. Within it lies the secret of love, but will never be penetrated, and all because it wouldn't be proper."

—*Laura Esquivel,* Like Water for Chocolate, *1989*

"For the historian, as distinct from the critic of art, the chocolate-box is one of the most significant products of our age, precisely because of its role as a catalyst."

—*Ernst Gombrich,* Listener, *February 15, 1979*

"Even though I have forgotten her
I continue to eat
plum after plum."

—*James Tipton*

"For those who love it, cooking is at once child's play and adult joy. And cooking done with care is an act of love."

—*Craig Claiborne,* Craig Claiborne's Kitchen Primer, *1969*

"Sex is good, but not as good as fresh sweet corn."

—*Garrison Keillor*

"The way to a man's heart is through his stomach."

—*Fanny Fern*

"Anybody who believed that the way to a man's heart is through his stomach flunked geography."

—*Robert Byrne*

"That's the way Chinese mothers show they love their children, not through hugs and kisses but with stern offerings of steamed dumplings, duck's gizzards, and crab."

—*Amy Tan,* The Joy Luck Club, *1989*

"Couples who cook together stay together. (Maybe because they can't decide who'll get the Cuisinart.)"

—*Erica Jong*

"Nothing takes the taste out of peanut butter quite like unrequited love."

—*Charlie Brown in the cartoon "Peanuts,"*
created by Charles Schulz

"It's funny that people think a healthy, firm, vibrant body is sexy, but they don't relate the same principle to a vegetable."

—*Marilu Henner,* Healthy Life Kitchen, 2000

"I've always seen that food and passion are synonymous."

—*Harvey Weinstein*

"Her breath is like honey spiced with cloves,
Her mouth delicious as a ripened mango."

—*Kumaradadatta,* Srngarakarika, *twelfth century*

"A plenteous meal may produce voluptuous sensations."

—*Marquis de Sade*

"Love: A word properly applied to our delight in particular kinds of food; sometimes metaphorically spoken of the favorite objects of all our appetites."

—*Henry Fielding*

"Passion in man is generally coexistent with a hankering after the pleasures of the palate."

—*Mahatma Gandhi,* An Autobiography: The Story of My Experiments with Truth, *1948*

"To as great a degree as sexuality, food is inseparable from imagination."

—*Jean-François Revel*

"Great food is like great sex—the more you have the more you want."

—*Gael Greene*

"[New England] oysters—straightforward, simple, capable of spirit but unadorned, like a Low Church service or a Boston romance."

—*M. F. K. Fisher, in* Smithsonian, *January 1988*

"Cooking, like unrequited love, is all in the mind. Once a girl has a decided her ex-boyfriend is a fat slob, she can forget all about him. It is just the same with burned cakes."
—*Madeleine Bingham*

"The critical time in matrimony is breakfast-time."
—*A. P. Herbert,* Uncommon Law, *1935*

"You can tell how long a couple has been married by whether they are on their first, second, or third bottle of Tabasco."
–*Bruce R. Bye*

"There is no sight on earth more appealing than the sight of a woman making dinner for someone she loves."
—*Thomas Wolfe*

"My mother always told me you could assess someone's sexual abilities by the way they ate asparagus. . . . After much experimentation, I have found my mother to be totally accurate."
—*Clarissa Dickson Wright,* Food, *1999*

"Cooking is like love. It should be entered into with abandon or not at all."

—Harriet Van Horne, Vogue, October 15, 1956

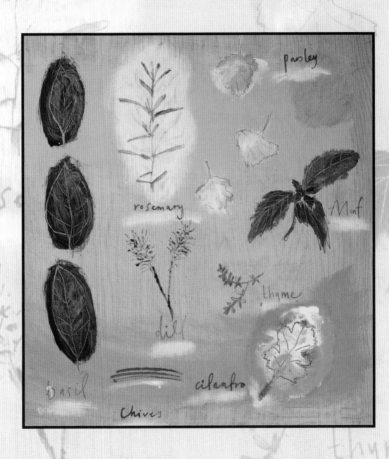

parsley

rosemary

Mint

thyme

basil

dill

cilantro

Chives

"The mere mention of the word 'aphrodisiac' conjures up visions of oysters in most minds."

—*Greg and Beverly Frazier,* Aphrodisiac Cookery, *1970*

"Eating takes a special talent. Some people are much better at it than others. In that way, it's like sex, and as with sex, it's more fun with someone who really likes it. I can't imagine having a lasting friendship with anyone who is not interested in food."

—*Alan King*

"After a perfect meal we are more susceptible to the ecstasy of love than at any other time."

—*Dr. Hans Bazli*

"The process of making onion soup is somewhat like learning to love . . . commitment, extraordinary effort, time, and [it] will make you cry."

—*Ronni Lundy, in* Esquire, *March 1984*

"Without bread, without wine, love is nothing."

—*French proverb*

"Madam, I have been looking for a person who disliked gravy all my life; let us swear eternal friendship."
—*Sydney Smith, in Lady S. Holland's* A Memoir of the Reverend Sydney Smith, *1855*

"Just as lovers know the time for intimate relations is approaching from the closeness and smell of their beloved, or from the caresses exchanged in previous love play, so Pedro knew from those sounds and smells, especially the smell of browning sesame seeds, that there was a real culinary pleasure to come."
—*Laura Esquivel,* Like Water for Chocolate, *1992*

"The aroma of good chili should generate rapture akin to a lover's kiss."
—*Motto of the Chili Appreciation Society International*

"Aphrodisiacs have occupied the searches and researches of man from ancient to modern times, and almost no culture, primitive or civilized, is without its pharmacopoeia of love foods."
—*Greg and Beverly Frazier,* Aphrodisiac Cookery, *1970*

"Eternity is two people and a roast turkey."

—*James Dent*

"'Suppose you're married and you love your wife, but you've fallen in love with another woman . . .'

"'I'm sorry, but I really can't understand that. I mean it's . . . just as incomprehensible to me as if, after having eaten a good dinner now, I were to go into a baker's shop and steal a roll.'

"Oblonsky's eyes sparkled more than usual.

"'Why not? Rolls sometimes smell so good that you can't resist them.'"

—*Leo Tolstoy,* Anna Karenina, *1877*

"Love doesn't just sit there, like a stone; it had to be made, like bread, remade all the time, made new."

—*Ursula K. Le Guin*

"Marriage, as I have often remarked, is not merely sharing one's fettuccine but sharing the burden of finding the fettuccine restaurant in the first place."

—*Calvin Trillin*

"I'm at the age where food has taken the place of sex in my life. In fact, I've just had a mirror put over my kitchen table."

—*Rodney Dangerfield*

"I cannot separate eroticism from food and see no reason to do so. On the contrary, I want to go on enjoying both as long as strength and good humor last."

—*Isabel Allende,* Aphrodite:
A Memoir of the Senses, *1998*

"While Venus fills the heart (without heart really)
Love, though good always, is not so good,
Ceres presents a plate of vermicelli,—
For love must be sustain'd like flesh and blood,—
While Bacchus pours out wine, or hands a jelly:
Eggs, oysters, too, are amatory food;
But who is their purveyor from above
Heaven knows,—it may be Neptune, Pan, or Jove."

—*George Gordon, Lord Byron,* Don Juan, *1824*

"Anyone who eats three meals a day should understand why cookbooks outsell sex books, three to one."

—L. M. Boyd